Praise for *Decoding You*

God speaks to us in many ways. At t
Word, through a prophet, through nature, through a circumstance, or even in a still small voice as we pray. He also speaks to us through dreams. In his book, *Decoding Your Spiritual Dreams,* Bryan Carraway brings an insightful yet practical approach to understanding how God speaks, how to properly interpret the message of the dream, as well as how to apply the revelation to one's life. This book will be a reference tool you will use for many years to come.

Jane Hamon, Pastor
Vision Church at Christian International
Santa Rosa Beach, FL

If you are interested in understanding how God speaks, you will want to read this book. God speaks today through His Word, through His people, and yes, even through your dreams. With a commitment to scripture and an equal passion for hearing God, Bryan Carraway has done a great service for the body of Christ. Read it and grow forward!

Dr. John Jackson, President
William Jessup University
Rocklin, CA

Bryan Carraway has done a wonderful job producing a prophetic work that addresses questions believers have wanted answered for years. *Decoding Your Spiritual Dreams* is not just a book on dream symbols, but Carraway digs deep into scripture with the skill of a gifted teacher and a seasoned interpreter of dreams to uncover the great mysteries of the night. This book truly breaks new ground in dream interpretation.

Dr. Charles R. Fox, Jr., Senior Pastor
Christ Community Church
Bowie, MD

In this book, *Decoding Your Spiritual Dreams,* the author takes this often-neglected topic and meets it head-on with a brilliant combination of biblical rootedness, theological integrity, and practical application. He provides us with tools for understanding these mysterious, subjective experiences we all have, called dreams, but always calls us back to subjecting our experiences to the standard of God's word and purposes. Whether it's read by a pastor, scholar, or a new believer, the wisdom of Carraway's book will meet them right where they are.

Marc Santom, Family Ministries Pastor
Kempsville Presbyterian Church
Virginia Beach, VA

Everyone dreams, but few understand the biblical record and teaching on dreams. At last, Bryan Carraway has given us a pointed and well written book that should be of interest to every Christian. I highly recommend it.

Dr. Vinson Synan, Dean
Oral Roberts University
Graduate School of Theology & Ministry
Tulsa, OK

Dreams are amazing. I call them "miracle movies" from heaven. But just when I'm certain I've got the "code" down as to how to interpret my dreams, I then have the next dream and I'm clueless again. I've found I must rely on those who've spent a lifetime learning the art and science of dreams. Beyond that, such people have been gifted with the discernment to take my dreams, and yours, and turn them into a real life word from God. Now, in *Decoding Your Spiritual Dreams,* Bryan Carraway has done it again. Bryan's book is a "decoding master key" for the dreamer. Use it to understand what God is saying to you! Get this book. And get one for a friend.

Steve Shultz, Founder
The Elijah List
Albany, OR

Pastors are often handed dreams to interpret. Like Nebuchadnezzar's court, we look into the eyes of inquiring parishioners, not knowing what to say. Like Daniel, Bryan Carraway has the gift not only to interpret dreams but to help us learn how as well. Get ready to dive deep; learn to uncover both the symbolism and mechanisms for discerning the voice of God in your dreams!

Dr. Antipas Harris, President
GIELD, Inc. &
The Urban Renewal Center, Dean
Norfolk, VA

Also by Bryan Carraway

Spiritual Gifts: Their Purpose & Power

Additional Resources

For additional resources or to invite Bryan to minister at your church, conference, or retreat please visit
www.bryanpaulcarraway.com

DECODING YOUR SPIRITUAL DREAMS

DECODING YOUR SPIRITUAL DREAMS

Keys for Christian Dream Interpretation

BRYAN CARRAWAY

XULON PRESS

Xulon Press
2301 Lucien Way #415
Maitland, FL 32751
407.339.4217
www.xulonpress.com

© 2017 by Bryan Carraway

Edited by Xulon Press.

All rights reserved solely by the author. The author guarantees all contents are original and do not infringe upon the legal rights of any other person or work. No part of this book may be reproduced in any form without the permission of the author. The views expressed in this book are not necessarily those of the publisher.

Unless otherwise indicated, Scripture quotations taken from the Holy Bible, New International Version (NIV). Copyright © 1973, 1978, 1984, 2011 by Biblica, Inc.™. Used by permission. All rights reserved.

Printed in the United States of America.

ISBN-13: 9781545611708

Acknowledgments

I WANT TO THANK SEVERAL friends who read over the early draft and helped me make improvements. These friends are: Leon Dunning, Marc Santom, and Dr. Gary Roberts. My wonderful wife, Pauline, also read the completed manuscript and offered very helpful comments enabling me to refine my message. I would also like to thank Joseph Cicero for editing this work.

I dedicate this book to my late mother, Janice Spriggs Ward, who was also a dreamer. We enjoyed many years of sharing our dreams with one another and marveling at this unique way that God speaks to His people.

Preface

FOR OVER TWENTY YEARS I have had the wonderful privilege of speaking in churches across the country. Wherever I am, my goal is always the same: deposit a word of teaching and exhortation to God's people—something that will enable them to serve Jesus more effectively.

There are so many messages we need to hear; so many that contribute to the building up of the body of Christ. We need those teachings on reaching our destiny, on developing godly character, and those exhortations on overcoming life's challenges. Do any of us ever really arrive at a place in God where we no longer benefit from an anointed message on faith? I know I've heard many sermons on all of these topics, and I am more equipped because of them.

As we grow in our walk with Christ, we pick up spiritual tools along the way—useful skills and understandings that take us to a new level in our Christian development. Some of these tools are "add-ons." If you happen to collect some along the way, you're better for it, but if you miss them, you can still have a pretty successful Christian life. Some tools, however, are foundational. If you fail to pick these up, their absence will create some noticeable deficiencies in your Christian walk. Spiritual tools don't affect your salvation. They just make it a whole lot easier to live it out.

I firmly believe that one of the foundational tools we must teach every Christian is how to hear the voice of the Lord. The Bible reveals that God speaks in many ways, each unique and wonderful. One of those ways is through our dreams. Let's not be uninformed about something so foundational.

I don't know what motivated you to pick up this book, but whatever your reason, I am glad you did. If you already have the understanding that God speaks in dreams, then my hope is that after reading this book, you'll be even more skilled in understanding them. If, on the other hand, you've never really considered that God speaks this way, then after you close this book's final page, I hope you will think I've presented a convincing argument. During the process, my desire for you is to pick up another spiritual tool which will help you live a more focused life for our Lord Jesus.

Socrates once said, "The unexamined life is not worth living." I feel that way about dreams. A spiritual dream left uncoded is like a letter from God left unopened. Join me as we take a deeper look into what the scriptures say about this mysterious way that God speaks. Never leave a message from God unanswered just because you are not familiar with the packaging it arrives in.

Grace and peace to you,

Bryan Carraway
Virginia Beach, Virginia
July 2017

Contents

Acknowledgements ix
Preface xi

Chapter 1:   One Dreamer to Another 1
Chapter 2:   A Survey of Dreams Throughout History 9
Chapter 3:   What the Bible Teaches About Dreams 21
Chapter 4:   Why God Speaks in Mysteries and Symbols... 47
Chapter 5:   Natural Dreams, Spiritual Dreams,
             Dark Dreams 59
Chapter 6:   Principles for Successful Dream
             Interpretation 72
Chapter 7:   Common Symbols in Spiritual Dreams 98
Chapter 8:   Inviting God into the World of Your Dreams . 136
Chapter 9:   Protocol for Dream Interpreters 141
Chapter 10: Case Studies: 7 Dreams Decoded 152

Afterword 177
Glossary 179
Appendix I: A Selection of Biblical Dreams 183
Appendix II: Questions & Answers 185
Appendix III: Reflection Questions for Group Study .. 191
Notes 195

Chapter 1

One Dreamer to Another

A Dream That Changed my Life

I HAD THE GOOD FORTUNE of growing up in a small town during my high school years. Like so many places in rural America, my hometown was like a portrait straight out of Mayberry. We had exactly one stop light, one grocery store, and one restaurant. If you happened to be passing through for lunch and didn't like greasy hamburgers from "Larry's," well then, you didn't eat.

A nice benefit of living in a small town is that everyone knows everyone else. It's comforting being part of such a community. We may not know one another well, but we wave when passing by. That is about how well I knew the family of which I am about to speak. It was not a close relationship by any means, but I knew them by name. We'll call this family "the Millers."

One night as a young man, I drifted off to sleep and had a dream of amazing clarity. In the dream, I was walking down a street when something caught my peripheral vision. I turned to see Mr. and Mrs. Miller on the roof of their house. I thought that was strange. I then noticed part of the roof had been greatly damaged. There were exposed beams, scattered shingles in the yard, and a huge portion of the roof was completely missing.

Upon further notice, I could see Mr. Miller with a hammer in his hand. Mrs. Miller had some type of tool in her hand, too. Both of them were on the roof repairing it. Then I noticed the Miller's daughter and oldest son were on the roof as well. The family toiled together to repair their damaged home.

I could not help but see the deep sadness etched across their faces. It was a terrible brokenness. They toiled to repair the damage, but it was obvious there was no joy in their labors. Then I awoke. I was very moved by the dream. It affected me at a deep level, so I reflected on it for a while before getting out of bed.

It was then I recalled their youngest son, about nineteen years old, was missing from the dream. That omission stood out to me and caused me to ponder further what this could possibly mean. I knew it portended something dark, but I was not entirely clear on its meaning. I just know it moved me like few dreams had before. You can imagine the shock and sadness I felt when a few weeks later I heard—along with the rest of our community—that Mr. and Mrs. Miller's youngest son committed suicide.

After much anguish and reflection, I knew that God had given me that dream a few weeks before. It was a message from heaven, but not realizing how God spoke through dreams, I was puzzled intellectually, but didn't really have a framework and understanding to know that I could petition the Lord to repeal what I had seen. It is a lesson I have never forgotten, and a mistake I have rarely repeated.

God has since opened my mind to better understand the dreams and visions that His people receive. I now understand that houses almost always represent people. The house in this dream represented not one life, but the collective life of that family unit. The roof had a massive hole in it, as if it had been suddenly and violently ripped away.

The broken condition of the roof was obviously a negative symbol, and the distressed faces of the family members was clearly an indication that something tragic had happened, or was soon to happen, in the life—or to "the house"—of that family. Because the youngest son was unaccounted for after the violent ripping away, it became clear that he was the one the dream was highlighting.

Over the years, I've had other prophetic dreams regarding similar dangers involving individuals, churches, or organizations. I now know dreams like these are given to Christians so we might intercede ahead of traumatic events, and that through prayer, these events can sometimes be avoided completely. When I hear these kinds of dreams today, I often have the insight to find God's cryptic message within. In those early days, however, I was just learning; and as you see, I didn't always understand the revelation I was given. I want to share with you what God has taught me over many years of interpreting dreams. I hope it will help you better understand your own dreams, so you are equipped to help those around you.

A Hunger for More Understanding

I am so thankful for the rich spiritual heritage in my family. Both my grandfather and great-grandfather were life-long Baptist pastors. I was raised in solid, Bible-believing churches all of my life, and yet, growing up I never once heard a sermon, a teaching, or even had a single Sunday School lesson on the subject of dreams. Some of my friends who were raised in Pentecostal or charismatic churches tell me similar stories. It seems that dreams have not always been valued or talked about much in church. I'm thankful that is slowly changing as more Christians come to understand the purpose God has for dreams.

That prophetic dream I had long ago about the young man who took his own life shook me so deeply that I soon began a personal study of God's word. I had to find out exactly what the scriptures taught about dreams and dreaming. During my study, I was amazed at how much material was devoted to the subject of dreams in the pages of the Bible.

I was pleasantly surprised to discover that God didn't just give dreams to special people like prophets and kings, but He gave dreams to everyday normal believers like you and me. I was overjoyed to learn that both the Old and New Testament teach that God desires to speak to His people regularly in dreams. Dreams are a common way He communicates to us about our lives, our families, and our future.

A Young Boy's Call

Vivid dreams have been a part of my life for as far back as I can remember. I began getting a series of prophetic dreams about my vocational future around age five. These dreams continued until I was eight or nine years old. As a young boy, I had recurring dreams of seeing myself teaching and preaching to groups of similarly aged young boys and girls. This, of course, symbolized that God had plans for me to be a teacher and an equipper to my generation.

When I had these dreams, I remembered they made an impression on me but I quickly forgot them and went on with my daily life. I'd be dishonest if I said I truly grasped them or was even excited about them. I mean, how excited can you get a five-year-old by saying, "Guess what, Bryan, you're gonna be a preacher!" I, like most other five-year-olds, had heroes, but they certainly were not preachers. When I grew up, I wanted to be an army man, a ninja, or an astronaut. Years later, at the age of 16, God revealed to me His call on my life. I knew part of my life's mission was to be spent encouraging God's people and teaching and preaching His holy word.

When I was 16, God began opening doors for me to preach and lead services in churches throughout East Texas and the surrounding region. When opportunities presented themselves to share His word, I was thrilled beyond measure (and I'm still thrilled doing it today). I discovered I loved studying the scriptures and mining out its rich truths. I loved seeing the lights go on in people's eyes as they received revelation of biblical truths that would change their lives forever.

It was then that I remembered the dreams of my childhood, and I was amazed they were now actually coming true. God had looked ahead through time and space and had given me a little peek at part of my destiny. When opportunities came before me, I would know not to turn to the right or the left, but instead stay straight in line with the purposes He had foreordained.

Think about it. God will give divine revelatory information to His people, through a dream, for their personal benefit. Then we, in faith, use that revelation to ensure we hit the mark He has for us.

Does it get any better than that? When we receive spiritual dreams from God, we know beyond a shadow of a doubt that we serve an all-knowing, sovereign God who is infinitely interested in us as an individual. So much so that He takes the time to craft a personal message to us and lays it softly in our minds at night as we rest.

Helping Others with Their Dreams

As I mentioned, I tend to dream quite often and usually remember many of them. During my early journey of learning about dreams, I also discovered something else. While many of my family and friends would comment on how confused they were by their strange dreams, that didn't seem to be my experience.

On the contrary, beginning in my teenage years, I noticed that I, too, would have strange dreams from time to time, but upon waking, I seemed to know what they meant. I was able to decode the symbolism of my dreams and arrive at the clear meaning of the message. Sometimes these dreams would instruct me to pray for specific individuals. Other dreams would give me insights into issues I was praying about. Some would even alert me to people that I would minister to in the future yet had not actually met.

I found all of this information very valuable and soon began to see these dreams as little gifts from God. I also noticed that when others told me of their dreams, I could often decode them as well and offer an interpretation they found extremely helpful in their present circumstances.

It is such a blessing to see new life return to the eyes of someone whose longstanding prayer request has finally been answered—in a dream. It's so rewarding to hear the gratitude in someone's voice when you've been able to assist with an interpretation that literally breaks a bondage that's hung over them for years. That, dear friends, is the power of dreams.

God has allowed me a unique opportunity to be invited into the private dream world of His choice servants. I take that trust very seriously. For over twenty years now, I've had the privilege of helping others with difficult dreams. For most of the last twenty years, I purposely kept my gift under the radar and ministered through it primarily for the benefit of my friends, family, and co-workers. It's not that I didn't enjoy using this gift. I truly find dreams fascinating, and I really enjoy laboring with others to help them understand theirs.

Then why keep this gift purposely quiet, you may ask? Well, two reasons. The first reason was the fact that dreams are not well respected in some Christian circles. There are many believers who say paying attention to dreams is foolish nonsense at best, or New Age and cultic at worst. These people have obviously not read the many passages in scripture that speak positively about dreams or the role God designed for them.

Fearful of appearing naïve in front of some circles, I kept the exercise of this particular gift directed toward those I trusted most. Looking back, that was nothing but my pride. I should have been more vocal back then about my ability to help others. Thankfully, our Lord still works through us even though we are all works in progress.

The second reason I didn't publicize the gift was the desire to avoid being labeled your friendly neighborhood "dream guy." I knew a story of a well-known minister who made it a policy of teaching on dream interpretation publically. For a long while after, he was inundated by requests from people to interpret their dreams. When I heard about his situation, I had concerns about a similar fate.

For example, here I am at the office Christmas party. Up walks a man, and before I have a chance to finish my punch and cake, he starts in, "Hey, you that dream guy? Say, I had the strangest dream last night of a goat with a snake's head that comes up behind me and starts eating my feet, only my feet are golden and the snake-goat can't eat 'em, so he just starts biting me. What does that mean?" My fantasy reply: "It means you're a weirdo, now leave me alone!"

So, yes, I had visions of being on 24/7 "dream duty." Reflecting back over the years, I'd have to say that most people are courteous, respectful, and genuinely just looking for anybody that can help them make sense of a disturbing or perplexing dream. I know I've had many of them myself, and if I were in their shoes, I'd probably want some help too. I am in their shoes; I've still got a few weird dreams that I do not fully understand.

So, that is why I did not speak publically about my experience with dreams until a few years ago when I wrote a series of articles on dream interpretation for a major Christian ministry's website. I'll never forget, soon after the articles were posted, I was contacted by the ministry's website director. He told me the articles were extremely popular, having received tens of thousands of views.

I wish I could claim the articles were popular because they were so well written, but the truth is: they were popular because they *met a need.* God's people were hungry for information on what the Bible taught about dreams and how they could better understand theirs. It was then I realized what I already instinctively knew—this was an area where we, as teachers, had not fully equipped God's people. It was time to correct that.

I promise you that the Word of God teaches that some dreams really do come from God, and He gives them to you because He loves you and has a message for you. I believe that you can interpret 90 percent of those dreams yourself. It just takes prayer, patience, and a willingness to learn the language of dreams and how God uses them. For the other 10 percent of your dreams, you will be pleased to know that God is still giving the gift of dream interpretation.

I know because I've experienced this grace operating in my own life, and I know that there are others in the body of Christ called to a similar ministry. Many of these men and women are more anointed in interpreting dreams than I am, and I am so thankful for the gift of God that flows within them. As the apostle Peter reminds us, *"Each one should use whatever gift he has received to serve others, faithfully administering God's grace in its various forms"* (1 Peter 4:10).

Our Journey Together

Let us now begin our journey together to better understand these mysterious messages given to us in the night. Allow me to give you a brief overview of how we'll proceed.

Chapter 2—Before we dig into the details of this study, we will take a few moments to conduct a historical survey of dreams. You may be surprised at how prominently dreams are mentioned in both secular and sacred history.

Chapter 3—Here we will gain a theological framework for our study, and we'll learn what the Bible has to say about dreams. We'll also examine the ten most common types of spiritual dreams that people receive.

Chapter 4—This chapter examines the most common question that I hear, which is, "Why does God use all these symbols instead of just speaking with us plainly?"

Chapter 5—In this section, we will consider the important issue of discerning which dreams are from God and which ones were caused by the pizza we had the night before.

Chapter 6—Here we'll explore the basic principles involved in understanding the symbolic nature of dreams.

Chapter 7—Here you'll get a dream interpretation "cheat sheet" because I have found some very common symbols that are universal. When you run into these, you'll have a head start in interpreting your dreams.

Chapter 8—This chapter will provide you with some specific tools to cultivate spiritual dreams in your life.

Chapter 9—This chapter is dedicated to those who feel a calling to interpret dreams. In this section, I share some best practices, and I exhort you to join me in exercising this gift with the integrity and accountability it requires.

Chapter 10—In this chapter I share some actual dreams which I have received from people over the years. I then provide the full interpretation I gave for the dream, along with additional comments that I believe you'll find helpful.

Chapter 2

A Survey of Dreams Throughout History

DREAMS HAVE PLAYED A pivotal role in the lives of great men and women, both Christian and non-Christian, throughout history. It's truly amazing to consider the sheer scope of their influence. Dreams have been used to warn leaders of assassination attempts, enabled scientists to arrive at major breakthroughs in their fields, and were the creative impetus behind many of the world's most beloved films, books, and musical recordings. Dreams are, in many ways, the silent partner behind some of the greatest discoveries and achievements in the modern age. They are also silent prophets, foretelling events dark and catastrophic that turn the tide of human history.

Dreams in Politics

Most students of history can recite details about the ill-fated events that happened April 14, 1865, as the Lincolns sat in State Box 7 of the Ford Theater. It was there that John Wilkes Booth changed history by firing a single-shot, round-ball .44 caliber Derringer, point-blank range, into President **Abraham Lincoln's** (1809–1865) head. What many may not know is the dream experienced by the sixteenth President of the United States almost two weeks prior to the assassination—a dream he shared three days before his death with his wife and a few friends.

Ward Hill Lamon, one of those friends, later related the President's fateful words:

> *About ten days ago, I retired very late. I had been up waiting for important dispatches from the front. I could not have been long in bed when I fell into a slumber, for I was weary. I soon began to dream. There seemed to be a death-like stillness about me. Then I heard subdued sobs, as if a number of people were weeping. I thought I left my bed and wandered downstairs. There the silence was broken by the same pitiful sobbing, but the mourners were invisible. I went from room to room; no living person was in sight, but the same mournful sounds of distress met me as I passed along. I saw light in all the rooms; every object was familiar to me; but where were all the people who were grieving as if their hearts would break? I was puzzled and alarmed. What could be the meaning of all this? Determined to find the cause of a state of things so mysterious and so shocking, I kept on until I arrived at the East Room, which I entered. There I met with a sickening surprise. Before me was a catafalque, on which rested a corpse wrapped in funeral vestments. Around it were stationed soldiers who were acting as guards; and there was a throng of people, gazing mournfully upon the corpse, whose face was covered, others weeping pitifully. 'Who is dead in the White House?' I demanded of one of the soldiers, 'The President,' was his answer; 'he was killed by an assassin.' Then came a loud burst of grief from the crowd, which woke me from my dream. I slept no more that night; and although it was only a dream, I have been strangely annoyed by it ever since.*[1]

The night before the Ides of March assassination of **Julius Caesar** (100–44 BC), then ruler of the mighty Roman Empire,

Calpurnia Pisonis (his third wife), dreamed about her husband being stabbed. Caesar himself also dreamed that he was flying above the clouds, shook hands with the god Jupiter, and was cast down headlong, foreshadowing the tragic death that happened on March 15th at the hands of a group of Roman senators.[2]

Osman I (1258—1324) was the leader of the Ottoman Turks and the founder of the dynasty that established and ruled the Ottoman Empire. The Empire, named after him, would prevail as a power for over six centuries. Before Osman I's birth, his father dreamed of a spring of water pouring from his house, building to such a torrential force that it eventually flowed over the earth. Terrified, the father shared the details with a local interpreter of dreams.[3]

"Take confidence," said the seer, "for your family has the blessing of God. You will soon have a son whom you shall behold as the founder of a monarchy which shall embrace all the countries of the world." "Osman's Dream," in fact, is an Old Turkish epic poem attributed to Osman I concerning a dream he had that pointed to the rise and growth of the empire long before the events actually happened. The Ottomans attached great importance to this dream of the founder of their empire.

Dreams in Science

Otto Loewi (1873–1961) was a German born physiologist who won the Nobel Prize for medicine in 1936 for his work on the chemical transmission of nerve impulses. As early as 1903, he believed, instead of the generally accepted theory of an electrical transmission of the nervous impulse, that it might be a chemical transmission. However, for two decades he could not prove his own theory.

Then in 1923, he had a dream that he later described in vivid detail: "The night before Easter Sunday of that year I awoke, turned on the light, and jotted down a few notes on a tiny slip of paper. Then I fell asleep again. It occurred to me at 6 o'clock in the morning that during the night I had written down something most important, but I was unable to decipher the scrawl. The next night, at 3 o'clock, the idea returned. It was the design of an experiment to determine whether or not the hypothesis of chemical transmission that I had uttered 17 years ago was correct. I got up immediately, went to the laboratory, and performed a single experiment on a frog's heart according to the nocturnal design." [4]

It took Loewi a decade to carry out a decisive series of tests to satisfy his critics, but ultimately, the result of his initial dream-induced experiment became the foundation for the theory of chemical transmission of the nervous impulse and led to being awarded the Nobel Prize 1936. He has since been referred to as the "Father of Neuroscience."

Frederick Banting (1891–1941) was a Canadian medical scientist and doctor who won the 1923 Nobel Prize in Medicine (with John James Rickard Macleod) as one of the co-discoverers of insulin. He first studied divinity, then turned to medicine. After his mother died from the effects of diabetes, he began searching for a cure, but with little success.

Finally, frustrated with the lack of results, he fell asleep, dreamed of the solution, and woke up understanding exactly the experiments he needed to carry out to give the results.[5] This started the work that led to the discovery of insulin, a hormone that regulates the sugar in the blood and helps in the treatment of diabetes. Before this, for thousands of years, contracting diabetes meant wasting away to a certain death. Frederick Banting's discovery changed that.

Danish physicist **Niels Bohr** (1885–1962) made foundational contributions to understanding atomic structure and quantum mechanics. Another dreamer who also won a Nobel, Bohr received the Nobel Prize in Physics in 1922. This accomplished scientist also worked at the top-secret Los Alamos laboratory in New Mexico on the Manhattan Project.

His inspiration came from a dream. Already increasingly well-known for his amazing skill in understanding the most challenging problems in the world of physics, he was nonetheless struggling with the structure of an atom, working through many designs, yet unsuccessful. In the midst of this struggle, one night he went to sleep, and in a vivid dream, he actually saw the nucleus of the atom with the electrons spinning around it, much like our solar system with the planets revolving around the sun. When he woke up, he realized through testing and experimentation that the dream was accurate. The Nobel Prize laureate often spoke openly about the dream that gave the answer.[6]

Albert Einstein (1879–1955), "The Father of Modern Physics," and Nobel Prize-winning theoretical physicist and philosopher, is regarded as one of the most influential and best known scientists and intellectuals of all time. His great intelligence and originality made the word "Einstein" synonymous with genius.

Any time he was asked about the theory of relativity, his most famous discovery, he unflinchingly attributed it to a dream he experienced in his youth. During that dream he was sledding down a mountainside, going faster and faster. As he flew down the hill he found himself watching the appearance of the stars change as he approached the speed of light, at which time the stars broke into fantastic colors. He said that the rest of his life was changed forever by that dream.[7]

The theory of relativity is still central to our understanding of the universe, and Einstein changed the political balance of power in the twentieth century through his scientific foundation in the development of atomic energy—all because of a dream.

Dreams in Business and the Arts

Robert Louis Stevenson (1850–1894) is the author of such classic books as *Treasure Island, Kidnapped,* and *Strange Case of Dr. Jekyll and Mr. Hyde*. Stevenson said the latter was conceived in a dream one night in 1885. "In the small hours," his wife later related, "I was awakened by cries of horror from Louis. Thinking he had a nightmare, I woke him. He said angrily, 'Why did you wake me? I was dreaming a fine bogey tale.'"[8]

Lloyd Osbourne, Stevenson's stepson and sometimes co-author, remembers, "I don't believe that there was ever such a literary feat before as the writing of Dr. Jekyll. I remember the first reading as if it were yesterday. Louis came downstairs in a fever; read nearly half the book aloud; and then, while we were still gasping, he was away again, and busy writing. I doubt if the first draft took so long as three days."

Published in 1886, the book became an instant classic, compulsively readable from its opening pages. In the first six months, 40,000 copies were sold. Queen Victoria read it. Sermons and editorials were written about it. When Stevenson and his family visited America a year later, they were mobbed by reporters at the dock in New York City. By 1901, it was estimated to have sold over a quarter-million copies, and today the dream-inspired *Strange Case of Dr. Jekyll and Mr. Hyde* is still considered one of the best tales ever written about the divided self.

The Guinness Book of World Records cites her as the first female American self-made millionaire. **Madame C.J. Walker** (1867–1919) created a cosmetics empire that blessed millions of people with her amazing beauty and self-care products.

Walker, an African-American woman, the daughter of former slaves, grew up extremely poor enjoying none of the benefits of well-connected society. What Madame C.J. Walker did have was an incredible work ethic and faith in God.

Her breakthrough came when she began experimenting with medicines and hair-care products to help with a scalp infection that caused her to lose most of her hair. She prayed to God for a solution. Little did she know, God would answer her, but He choose to give her the answer in a dream.

She would later famously recall that the solution to her hair loss came from a formula given to her by a man appearing in a dream. The man in her dream gave her a series of ingredients including instructions on how to mix it. Walker later recalled, "Some of the remedy was grown in Africa, but I sent for it, mixed it, put it on my scalp, and in a few weeks my hair was coming in faster than it had ever fallen out. I tried it on my friends; it helped them. I made up my mind to begin to sell it." [9]

Increasingly successful as she built Madam C.J. Walker Manufacturing Company from the ground up, she became an inspiration to all women and was well known as a philanthropist and social activist. At her death, she was considered to be the wealthiest African-American woman in America.

Two machines invented in the mid-1700s (the loom and the "Spinning Jenny") were influential in bringing about the Industrial

Revolution. **Elias Howe** (1819–1867) was committed to developing what he hoped would be the next major breakthrough, which was a sewing machine that could perform on par with the other two advances. As early as 1790, others had developed working sewing machines, even patenting their designs. Yet none had performed as Howe hoped his idea would.

As years went by, the biggest challenge remaining was the needle. His latest attempt was pointed on both ends with an eye for the thread in the middle. Then came a nightmare in which he was captured by a group of natives who placed him in a pot of boiling water as they danced around him, prodding him with sharp spears. In the dream, he noticed that all the spears had holes in the tips. Awaking with a start, he suddenly realized that what he had seen in his dream could provide the long-awaited answer to his challenge.[10]

When he developed a needle with the hole at one tip, the next step was developing the machine to make sure the thread could be caught after it went through the cloth. It worked remarkably well, and on September 10, 1846, Elias Howe received the first United States patent (U.S. Patent 4,750) for a sewing machine using the remarkable lockstitch design.

Dreams Throughout the History of the Church

As we just briefly surveyed together, dreams have played a unique role in the lives of notable people, both Christian and non-Christian. Dreams and dream interpretation (sometimes called oneiromancy), have been intricately woven into the fabric of civilization since the beginning of mankind. For millennia, dreams have been respected as a source of illumination as well as a medium of divine communication.

The ancient people of Mesopotamia, the Assyrians, the Chinese, and ancient Central American cultures all have literature devoted to dreams and their usefulness. Dreams are even mentioned in the ancient Egyptian *Letters to the Dead* texts, which were written over 2,000 years before Christ.

While guides to dreams have been found in the remains of numerous cultures, the largest and most complete compilation of dream information and teachings to survive from the ancient world is the Greek work entitled the *Oneirocritica (The Interpretation of Dreams)*. It was authored by Artemidorus of Daldis during the second century A.D. While these references to dreams from cultures past are fascinating to study, it's even more interesting to discover what role dreams have played in the lives of God's people through the ages.

Dreams in the Old Testament

Throughout the Old Testament dreams are mentioned numerous times, often prominently, and are portrayed as messages from God. The Jewish people recognized that God spoke in many ways, and dreams were just one of the avenues He made available for knowing His will. Below is a brief sample of some of the dreams mentioned in the Old Testament. Appendix I will provide a more complete summary for easy reference.

- **Genesis 15:1–21**—Abraham interacted with God and, while in a "deep sleep," was given a prophetic dream concerning God's covenant with the patriarch and future generations.
- **Genesis 20:1–18**—Abimelech was warned by God in a dream to avoid taking Abraham's wife Sarah.
- **Genesis 28:10–22**—God spoke to Jacob, showing him a ladder to heaven.
- **Genesis 37:5–11**—God gave Joseph dreams about his future and his family.
- **Genesis 40:1–19**—Joseph interpreted the dreams of the Pharaoh's imprisoned cupbearer and baker.
- **Genesis 41:1–40**—Joseph wisely interpreted the dreams of the Pharaoh of Egypt and was quickly appointed as second in command.
- **Judges 7:9–18**—Gideon overheard two enemy soldiers describing a dream and its interpretation prior to his surprise attack on the Midianites.
- **1 Kings 3:5–28**—Solomon was tested by the Lord with a question God asked him in a dream. His response in the

dream mirrored his heart's true desire, and upon waking, his life was changed forever.
- **Daniel 2:1–45**—After all the best-known wise men in the Chaldean kingdom were unable to interpret the king's dream, the Jewish captive Daniel reveals that the dream speaks of God's future coming Kingdom.

Dreams in the New Testament

The New Testament does not record near as many dreams as the Old Testament. However, there are several mentioned, including a specific promise in Acts 2:17–18 that dreams will continue throughout the church age as a means of divine communication. Here are a few of the dreams mentioned in the New Testament.
- **Matthew 2:1–12**—The wise men of the East were told in a dream to avoid King Herod on their journey home after seeing the infant Jesus.
- **Matthew 2:13–15**—Joseph was directed in a dream to flee with Mary and Jesus to safety in Egypt.
- **Matthew 2:19–21**—After Herod's death, Joseph is told in a dream to return to Israel.
- **Matthew 27:15–19**—Pontius Pilate's wife had a dream about Jesus' innocence and sent a message to her husband who was sitting in judgment over Him.

Dreams of a spiritual nature did not just end with the New Testament saints. The promise of Acts 2:17–18 is found to be true as we read the numerous accounts of dreams and visions recorded over the last two thousand years of church history.

Dreams in the Post-New Testament Age

Most of the church Fathers made at least some brief mention of dreams. Some commented on them extensively and showed a keen understanding of their place in the Christian's life. Dreams are mentioned by Justin Martyr, Irenaeus, and Clement. The highly respected **Origen** had this to say about dreams in his major apologetic work, *Against Celsus:*

> *We, nevertheless, so far as we can, shall support our position, maintaining that, as it is a matter of belief that in a dream impressions have been brought before the minds of many, some relating to divine things, and others to future events of this life, and this either with clearness or in an enigmatic manner—a fact which is manifest to all who accept the doctrine of providence.*[11]

Dreams are also respected in the writings of such men as Ambrose, Jerome, and **Augustine**. Interestingly, Augustine's own conversion was foretold to his mother Monica in a dream. She had been praying for her son when the Lord gave her a dream that pictured him serving Christ. Because of that dream, she found the strength to continue her intercessory prayers on his behalf. The dream proved prophetic because her son would later embrace Christ, and God would use his brilliant mind and make him one of the most influential thinkers the church has ever produced. This man would later be known to the entire world as the great Saint Augustine of Hippo.

Dreams have played a unique role in the lives of God's people throughout the centuries. One such example can be seen in the life of **Saint Patrick of Ireland** (387–493). Patrick was born into a wealthy family in Britain. Tragically, at age 16, he was taken prisoner by Irish raiders, brought to Ireland, and sold into slavery.

In his spiritual autobiography, the *Confessio,* Patrick recalls how, after enduring six years of captivity, God spoke to him in a dream. He heard a voice say, "Behold, your ship is prepared." He summoned the courage to flee his captors and, guided only by God, embarked on a 200-mile trek to the coast where he found a ship bound for Britain.[12] Already a devout follower of Christ, he entered the priesthood upon his return to Britain. However, his days in Britain were not to last. Patrick recalled another dream given to him just a few years after returning home that would draw him back to the country where he had been a captive:

> *"I saw a man coming, as it were from Ireland. His name was Victoricus, and he carried many letters, and he gave me one of them. I read the heading, 'The Voice of the Irish.' As I began the letter, I imagined in that moment that I heard the voice of those very people who were near the wood of Foclut, which is beside the western sea, and they cried out, as with one voice: 'We appeal to you, holy servant boy, to come and walk among us.'"* [13]

In 432, in obedience to the dream, he returned to Ireland, to the land of his captors. When Patrick returned, it was so that he, full of God's Spirit, could "set the captives free." God so blessed his nearly three decades of ministry there that it is often said Saint Patrick, almost singlehandedly, converted Ireland from a land of pagan Druid worshippers into a Christian nation.

Finally, **John Newton**, (1725–1807) a slave ship captain for many years, received a dream during one of his voyages that ultimately led to his conversion. It would plant a seed that would begin his life-changing journey. Newton recalled a dream that shook him so deeply he could hardly eat or conduct his business for two or three days afterward.

In his dream, a man appeared and gave him a golden ring of exceptional beauty and worth. He was told that as long as the ring was in his possession he would be successful and happy. A second man appeared, and mocking his belief in this ring, convinced him to throw it overboard. Newton did so, and the ring sank slowly to the bottom of the sea. The tempter then revealed that he had tricked Newton and that the ring encapsulated all of God's mercy and love. Accusing him, the second man said, "Yet you willingly threw it away."[14] At that moment, a massive fire burst out of a mountain range within Newton's sight, and he realized his folly, knowing swift judgment would soon be upon him.

In a turn of events, the first man reappeared, dove into the water, and retrieved his ring, giving Newton a second chance. That man then told Newton: "If you should be entrusted with this ring again, you would soon bring yourself into the same distress. You are not able to keep it, but I will preserve it for you, and, whenever it is needful, will produce it on your behalf."

Newton would later acknowledge the dream's divine origin, commenting that the ring, forfeited for a time to Satan's seduction, symbolized God's goodness and the gift of life. Newton would eventually give his heart to Christ, renounce the slave trade, and become a minister. He was also a prolific writer of hymns, including his most famous one, which is still sung in our churches today, "Amazing Grace." [15]

Chapter 3

What the Bible Teaches About Dreams

THE SINGLE MOST IMPORTANT passage in all of scripture regarding dreams is found in Job 33:14–18. The book of Job tells the story of a righteous servant of God who, through no fault of his own, endures a trial of suffering that is almost unimaginable.

Most of the book of Job centers around the dialogue of four friends, completely wrong but well intentioned, who've come to tell Job that he must be suffering due to some un-confessed sin in his life. However, one of his friends, Elihu, strikes theological gold when he makes an observation about the fact that God does speak, but His communications sometimes come in very unusual ways.

> *For God does speak, now one way, now another though man may not perceive it. In a dream, in a vision of the night, when deep sleep falls on men as they slumber in their beds, he may speak in their ears and terrify them with warnings, to turn man from wrongdoing and keep him from pride, to preserve his soul from the pit, his life from perishing by the sword.* Job 33:14–18

There it is. Scripture not only clearly states that God speaks to His people in dreams but, speaking through Elihu, the Holy Spirit also tells us one of the reasons He does so "to preserve our soul." We will explore some other purposes that God has for dreams in a moment, but first, let's briefly review the principal ways God chooses to communicate with His creation.

God Speaks in a Variety of Ways

God Speaks Through His Word

2 Timothy 3:16–17 informs us, *"All scripture is God-breathed and is useful for teaching, rebuking, correcting, and training in righteousness, so that the man of God may be thoroughly equipped for every good work."* The primary way God speaks to His people is through His word.

If we are serious about knowing the mind and heart of God, then we'll be serious about regularly reading and studying God's word. The Bible contains God's revelation about salvation, spiritual growth, and everything else we need to be fully established in Him. In the pages of the Bible we discover what God thinks about marriage, money, child raising, paying taxes, ministering through our gifts, and everything else.

If we will commit before the Lord to regularly read His word—asking Him to speak to us—He will. We'll then be able to discern His will for our life and be blessed. I love what Joshua 1:8 says, *"Do not let this book of the Law depart from your mouth; meditate on it day and night so that you may be careful to do everything written in it. Then you will be prosperous and successful."*

God Speaks Through His Holy Spirit

The apostle John records an interesting statement of Jesus' in John 10:4. Jesus tells His followers that, *"his sheep follow him because they know his voice."* The generation that walked and talked with Jesus actually heard His audible voice. In our generation today, we too can hear His voice, but it is the voice of His Holy Spirit. It's that still, small voice, that over time, we learn to distinguish from our own.

This voice speaks to us in the busyness of our days, calling us to pray for a co-worker. It's the same voice that prompts us to share about Jesus with the stranger on the bus. As we go about our lives and we quiet ourselves before Him, we come to rely on that voice to guide us, instruct us, and warn us. So this too, the very voice of God's Spirit, is a major way God communicates to His people.

God Speaks Through Others

God will often use another person to speak His will and purposes into our life. Think of all those times Paul spent with his young protégée, Timothy. God used this seasoned leader to speak life and destiny into this young boy. Timothy received the word of the Lord from Paul and grew up to be a mighty man of God and a successful pastor in the city of Ephesus. In Exodus 18:13–24, we see Moses' father-in-law, Jethro, being used by the Lord to give practical advice to Moses, so he will not wear himself out in the work of the ministry.

We should remind ourselves that there is an entire spiritual gift, the word of wisdom, which functions solely to dispense Spirit-directed advice to those who will receive it. I encourage you to be open to receiving a word of exhortation or instruction from whomever the source may be. A word may come from your spouse, a friend, or a church leader. It could come from someone you believe to be less spiritually mature than yourself. Nevertheless, God can use them to deliver a timely, accurate word.

God Speaks Through Prophetic Words

Another common way God speaks to His people is through prophetic words. When the Lord wishes to speak something very specific to us, He will often lay that message on the heart of someone else and have them deliver it to us. Paul exhorts us in 1 Thessalonians 5:20, "*do not treat prophecies with contempt.*" Apparently some in the church didn't care too much for prophecies, especially the ones that called them on their "stuff." I don't much like those kind either. If we want to grow up, it's not all pudding and cakes; we have to eat our vegetables too.

I'll never forget a prophetic word I received many years ago. The prophet reminded me of the godly men the Lord put in my life who taught me so much. He told me something I have never forgotten to this day. He said, "The Lord says, it was not *their voice* speaking to you, it was *My voice* speaking to you." He was right. God put some great men in my life who spoke words of life to me, but in reality, it was God's Spirit directing those men to teach me the lessons He previously taught them.

God Speaks Through Common Life Circumstances

In Jeremiah 18:1–10, the prophet Jeremiah is walking leisurely down a road. He turns to see a potter at work. As he watches this craftsman molding his vessel, the Spirit of God begins speaking to him about how God is very much like a potter on the wheel, molding and shaping the destiny of nations.

We need to realize God can speak very deep spiritual insights to us at a football game, after watching a movie, or while observing children at play. We need to be sensitive to understand that everything around us in creation, in society, and in our daily relationships are little lessons God wants to pour into us. The voice of the Lord speaking to our hearts this way is just as real and valid as when the Spirit shows us something in the Word or in a dream. May we have our spiritual antennas always on, ready to receive any truth the Holy Spirit may want to drop in our minds.

God Speaks Through Dreams and Visions

Finally, God speaks to people through dreams *and* visions. Visions are very similar to dreams; they both involve God giving us direct, but cryptic, revelation. The main difference is that visions occur when we are awake, while dreams occur in our sleep. These ancient forms of communication between God and man have been going on since the days of the patriarchs in the book of Genesis. In Acts 2:17–18, the apostle Peter proclaims that in the last days the

Holy Spirit will be poured out upon God's people in an unprecedented way. One of the benefits of this last-days outpouring will be an increase in dreams and visions. Peter shares:

In the last days, God says, I will pour out my Spirit on all people. Your sons and daughters will prophesy. Your young men will see visions, your old men will dream dreams. Even on my servants, both men and women, I will pour out my Spirit in those days, and they will prophesy.

Job 33:16–18 names just a few of the reasons why God gives dreams. He states that dreams are given to people to "terrify them with warnings," to "turn man from wrongdoing," and to "preserve his soul from the pit." Due to the context of the passage, Elihu is naturally focusing on the function of spiritual preservation through dreams. Thus, the few examples he mentions speak primarily of warning dreams and revelatory dreams. However, biblical dreams served many other functions as we'll soon see.

In fact, as we study scripture, we see many different types of dreams recorded for us. There is no biblical classification system offered in the pages of scripture to describe the many types of dreams found there. As we study all of the dreams found in the Bible, some common classifications emerge. These will be helpful to use for the purposes of our study. We'll now look at the ten most common types of spiritual dreams people receive from the Lord.

Types of Spiritual Dreams

Warning Dream

This is one of the most common types of dreams found in the Bible. Often God will give us a dream solely to warn us about an upcoming situation that will harm us emotionally, physically, or spiritually. Remember, dreams are given to us to "preserve our soul from the pit." Sometimes, a dream is the best way for God to get our attention—especially if He has tried other avenues and we've been unresponsive.

For instance, let's suppose Sarah and Mike have been married for nine years. They have their share of problems, but all in all, they've had a good marriage. They have three beautiful children, ages seven, five, and two. Mike is in the Navy and is often out to sea for nine months at a time. It's hard raising three kids alone, and discouragement and high stress have been taking their toll on Sarah for quite some time. She's tried to be a trooper, but honestly, she has not felt this low and spiritually dry in a long, long time. Let's say Mike's new promotion has been putting a lot of stress on him lately, and it seems all they do these days is argue about money, time with the kids, and everything else.

Mike should be doing a better job of holding Sarah and making time for her. He should be reassuring her that, when he gets back from his next assignment, they'll make some changes in the family. That is what Mike *should* have done on his last leave home. He didn't. Now he's away from the family again for another nine-month deployment.

Now let's say Sarah has been really encouraged by Jason, their son's baseball coach. Jason always seems to have time to talk. He even brought her a smoothie one day as she sat in the stands to watch her son practice. "Wow, what a nice guy. Mike never does those things for me anymore."

Fast forward two months. Sarah can't get Jason out of her mind. He's obviously interested. As a Christian, she shouldn't be entertaining the idea, but she is. She keeps finding excuses to be around him—even lingering around long after practice ended, so they can "talk."

Sarah's best friend confronted her last week. "Sarah, you've been spending way too much time around Jason. I think you've developed a crush on him. Girl, you need to back off. This leads to nowhere but trouble." Sarah appeases her, promises she'll back off and quit thinking of him, but can't follow through. Jason just happened to be driving through their neighborhood the other day and stopped by the house. He and Sarah talked in the doorway for a long while, but she never invited him in. Yep, she's got this all under control, no worries.

Sarah gets the kids fed and off to bed that night. She finally retires for the evening. Later that night, she has a vivid dream. In the dream, she and Jason declare their love for one another and are involved in a passionate encounter. For a while, everything is ecstasy until she arrives home to announce she is leaving with Jason and moving away.

In the dream, her kids are crushed. They're crying their eyes out, "Daddy, Daddy, I don't want to go!" She takes one look at her husband Mike, and he's a broken man. The affair has devastated him and killed his self-esteem. Sarah wakes up from the dream with the most God-awful feeling in the world. In the dream, she could actually *feel* the pain she caused her children. She could *feel* the broken heart of her husband.

All that day, she's in a spiritual depression. The dream felt so real. She just had a taste of what it would feel like the day after she broke her wedding vows. Sarah just had a wake up call. The message: *Do this and the price you'll pay is more severe than you can even imagine. Don't throw away a good marriage because of a temporary problem. Go to the Father.*

I can assure you, after one really vivid warning dream like that, Sarah will think twice about lingering after baseball practice again. In fact, she'll probably call her husband and set up a date night for when he returns, then call up her girlfriend to come over and cry with her and pray with her. She's just been saved by a heavenly wake up call.

The Shelf Life of "Wake Up" Calls (for when you're about to do something really stupid)

1. A thought in your head saying, "This is a really stupid idea"	3 hours of protection
2. Reading a scripture verse pertaining to your brand of stupidity	3 days of protection

3. A friend you respect scolds you, "Stop what you're doing!"	3 weeks of protection
4. A terrifying dream from God that shakes you to the core	3 months of protection

Warning dreams in scripture served pretty much the same purpose. As a matter of fact, I got the idea of the story about Sarah and Mike from a similar dream God gave Abimelech in Genesis 20:1–7. Abimelech had taken Sarah, Abraham's wife, and was about to "know her" in the biblical sense when God gave him a tailor-made warning dream that quickly killed his amorous intentions!

Warning dreams are given to protect us. We might be given a dream about a trap the enemy set for us or about a person that will soon be coming into our life who is not what they say they are. The dream is given so we'll be wise and stay in a spirit of prayer regarding the issue at hand. These dreams are extremely valuable, and we are wise when we heed their counsel.

Confirmation Dream

Have you ever given yourself to deep thought and reflection about something and wished you could just ask God what He thought about the matter and be done with it? Well, sometimes God will give you very clear insight into issues you've been thinking and praying about. Sometimes, He decides to reveal His thoughts on the subject through what I call "confirmation dreams."

Confirmation dreams are simply dreams in which God confirms an issue with you, letting you know that your judgments about a matter are correct or not. You can then move forward in confidence knowing you've rightly perceived the heart of God on the matter. Sometimes, confirmation dreams reveal God's choice between two options you've been considering. The dream will clearly point to one option being superior and serves as confirmation of God's will on the issue.

I'll never forget a confirmation dream I received once regarding spiritual warfare in the church. I had always been bothered by the fact that some Christians seem to be able to engage in successful spiritual warfare while others seem habitually weak and subject to the plundering of the enemy. I thought, "Why God? We all have the same Holy Spirit? Why such discrepancy in results from church to church?" I had my ideas of why this was so, but I was convinced I was right after a dream the Lord gave me.

In the dream, I was hunched over with a lot of other people. I knew these people were Christians. This was a time of war, and nearby, a battle was violently in progress. Everyone had huddled together out of fear. I remember our leader was being very passive. He didn't seem to have a plan for what to do. I finally went up to him and said, "If we wait here three or four years like this, we'll all be dead. We have to do something soon." I suggested to him that we should at least put on the uniform of the enemy and sneak over there. Hopefully, we could blend in and take some of them out in the process. I told him if we just continued to sit around, we would be picked off eventually.

Then, I noticed a white wool carpet rolling out, and upon it strutted out some man of authority. I perceived him to be one of our senior leaders, a general of ours. He was wearing a very old military uniform from the Revolutionary War era.

The scene changed, and I saw several superfast Concord jets fitted for military service racing above me. One of them had been shot down. I commented to someone nearby, "Let's just mass produce more of these." I remember thinking if we had a whole fleet of these, there was no way we could lose the war. I was then told by the gentleman that it is impossible to mass produce these special jets because each one had a unique design. Each fuselage was distinctively made, and their aerodynamics forced air to flow over each plane in a different way. I got the sense that they took a lot of time and skill to make, and that is why they could not be massed produced. Then, I woke up.

I interpreted this dream to be a picture of the spiritual warfare tactics going on in the church today. One part of the church is fighting passively using ancient tactics, while the other part is fighting an aggressive war using very sophisticated, powerful equipment. The old, antiquated method of spiritual warfare is based on ignorance. They don't know what to do or how to fight in this war. This is represented by the fact that the leader doesn't even totally realize that he's in a war in the first place. The people these pastors call "general" (their spiritual heroes and leaders) are archaic types, like the George Washington figure that made an appearance.

Some churches and some pastors don't understand demonic forces are loose on the earth today. They've never been taught how intercessors can break down strongholds over their churches and communities. They are not open to vital field intelligence via prophetic words or dreams and visions, which could be extremely useful to them. Instead, they simply go on having their Bible studies, pot luck dinners, and church work days, totally oblivious to the massive spiritual warfare taking place all around them. This is a war that claims the lives of their people year after year.

My suggestion to the leader indicated that sometimes we need to get over to where the enemy is—in his camp, in his world—and bring the fight to him. It also means that to win over those in the other world, we sometimes have to dress like them, meaning finding common ground. As Paul says, *"To the Jew I became like a Jew . . . to those not having the law I became like one not having the law"* (1 Corinthians 9:20–21a).

The Concord jets represent those in the church who have superior knowledge on how to engage in spiritual warfare. However, the preparation needed to do that kind of battle does not come quick and easy. It is not "mass-produced." The unique fuselage designs speak to individuality and, from years of allowing God to mold them (i.e. mold their fuselage), they have been made into powerful weapons in the Spirit. The way the Spirit moves over and through these men and women is unique, thus the unique "airflow" properties of each jet. There are no quick routes to becoming a Concord. It takes years of submission.

God can use a dream to confirm His desire for you to minister to a particular person. He may give a dream to confirm a theological issue you've been praying about. God used a vision to correct Peter's wrong theological understanding of the Gentiles in Acts 10:9–11:17. The applications are endless. Confirmation dreams will show us the mind and heart of God on a whole range of topics.

When we get them we can be sure that God has revealed His will to us in a more perfect way.

Encouragement Dream

One of the best encouragement dreams in scripture is found in 1 Kings 3:5–15. Young Solomon has before him the awesome task of leading the nation of Israel after his father, King David, died. While the thoughts of his future kingship weigh heavily on his mind, he drifts off to sleep.

In the dream, the Lord appears and says, "Ask for whatever you want me to give you." Solomon, instead of asking for wealth or other selfish desires, asks for the ability to rule wisely. We all know the story. He gets the wealth and a whole lot more because his response greatly pleased the Lord. In the dream, God promises to give him the requisite wisdom and will throw in riches and honor as well. How's that for an encouraging dream!

Solomon knew the dream he had was not just a dream from his own mind. He clearly recognized it as a divine dream. If we look closely in verse fifteen, we see Solomon's response, which proves this. After he awoke from the dream, he returned to Jerusalem, stood before the ark, and sacrificed burnt offerings and fellowship offerings. He called all of his court together and celebrated with a feast. Quite an appropriate response I'd say.

Encouragement dreams are given simply to let us know that God is with us, is pleased with us, and that He will not abandon us while we carry out our mission for Him. Sometimes we get discouraged in our lives and in the midst of the work of the Lord. Whenever our Father senses we need an extra boost of faith, He will often drop an encouragement dream in our spirit as we sleep. You'll know when you receive one of these dreams. Upon waking, you will have renewed determination and increased faith to continue the work God has called you to perform.

Calling Dream

I have found it is very common for God to speak to us about our future callings, sometimes years in advance. He often does this through a dream. Whenever we have a dream that depicts some aspect of our future ministry or some aspect of His will for our life, I like to label these "calling dreams."

We see a great example of a calling dream in Genesis 37:5–11. Joseph has a dream about sheaves of grain. He's so excited about this dream that he calls all of his family together to tell them about it. In his dream, his grain sheaf rose and stood upright. His brother's sheaves all bowed before his. He then goes on to relay another dream he has in which the sun, moon, and eleven stars all bow down before him. Joseph had 11 brothers. Hmm, I wonder who those eleven stars represent?

They seemed to venture a good guess that it was them, and they were not too enthused with their little brother's delusions of grandeur. As a matter of fact, an already rocky relationship went downhill after Joseph shared that dream. I believe Joseph was very unwise in sharing a dream like that. The dream can do little more than cause envy in most people, so why did Joseph share it? Probably because he was only 17 and a little immature.

The dream was indeed from the Lord, for it foretold Joseph's destiny as a governmental official. In time, thirteen years later to be exact, Joseph would be the second most powerful man in Egypt, and he would live long enough to see his brothers do exactly what the dream foretold: bow before him.

I'm convinced God gives us calling dreams for two primary reasons. First, they are given so we'll hold on and persevere when times get tough. We are to protect our calling and treat it as precious. We cannot discard it just because we don't see it fulfilled immediately. Oftentimes, God takes us to the desert to develop our character, to test us, and to put within us the experiences, people, and gifts we'll need to fulfill the calling dream He gave us years before.

Secondly, I believe the Lord gives us calling dreams so we will know which path to take in life. We'll know what opportunities, education, and work offers make sense for us based on the plans He has for us. In my mid-twenties, I finally finished my undergraduate degree having taken eight years to complete it. I was understandably tired, and while I was excited about the prospect of graduate school, there was still a little part of me that wasn't sure I really wanted to make that commitment.

What settled it for me was my firm conviction that part of my calling was to teach and preach God's word. I knew that to develop that call properly, I needed training at a much deeper level. I was convinced that teaching would be a major part of my ministry. I had that confirmed in the immediate years before seminary. Most importantly, I had it confirmed in those series of preaching dreams I had as a child. I now live and enjoy what I repeatedly saw myself doing in dreams—sharing God's word and seeing it change people from the inside out. Hallelujah!

Portrait Dream

The next type of dream we need to consider is what I call, "portrait dreams." As the name implies, this type of dream gives us a true picture—or portrait—of ourselves in regards to our spiritual, mental, or emotional health at the present moment. Portrait dreams are one of the most common types of spiritual dreams God gives. Over fifty percent of the spiritual dreams God will give you over the course of your life will likely be portrait dreams. Learn to recognize them now—you've been getting them all of your life and you'll be getting lots more.

The Lord Jesus is very interested in our hearts and how we do, or do not, guard them from the corrupting influences of the world. In the course of our daily lives, it's so easy to let bad attitudes and ways of thinking supplant what we know to be true in the Word of God. For example, we all have people that get on our nerves. Over time we build offenses and if we're not careful, we come to loathe or even despise others.

On the other hand, sometimes we're riding high spiritually. Our walk with God couldn't be stronger. We're prayed up and actively seeing God use us in our daily interactions. Perhaps we're ministering out of our own power in one particular area and God would have us trust His power for the situation at hand. All of these issues are perfect scenarios that might cause God to intervene with a portrait dream.

God-given portrait dreams show us a snapshot of our hearts, our level of faith, our current preconceived notions, or our thinking about some issue or person that we're presently dealing with. Think of portrait dreams as the equivalent of a good friend at a coffee shop making a comment about something you recently said or did, good or bad. Portrait dreams are exactly the same thing, except in this case, the creator of the universe is stopping by your bedroom and offering unsolicited commentary about something He's noticed you thinking or doing recently.

Let me share with you a portrait dream I received a few years ago. It was a dark, stormy night, and there was an eerie feel all around me. Out of nowhere, a shadowy demonic figure began attacking a group of people who were standing near me. In the dream the demon attempted to take me out so he could more easily get to the others, but he was unsuccessful. I was not quite powerful enough to defeat him, but neither was he powerful enough to defeat me.

The people around me were quite startled that this supernatural being had materialized in front of us, and we decided to remove ourselves from the open field and take shelter nearby. The dream ended with me and the others gathered in an old barn on this cold, dark night, waiting for this phantom menace to make his inevitable return. I had a sense in the dream that I was ready for the demon should he wish another round. The people around me had confidence as well that, if he returned, we were not going down easily.

I awoke and knew in my heart that it was a spiritual dream from the Lord, and yet it made no profound announcements in my life. It was not quite encouraging enough for me to label it an "encouragement dream," nor did I sense it pertained to any future situation in my life; thus, it was not a "prophetic dream." What the dream *did* do for me is this: It simply gave me a small picture of my actual spiritual power at that point in my life. The dream basically confirmed that I had a measure of spiritual power the demons of hell could not easily dismiss. I liked that dream. I personally choose to label that one in my dream journal as a "portrait dream."

When you have a spiritual dream of dark forces attacking you, and you're able to repel them, that's a portrait of your current spiritual health, or lack of health, depending on the outcome of the dream. When you dream of ministering to crowds of people and many of them are broken and crying out to God for salvation, guess what? That's a *great* dream. It's providing you a portrait of how God is using you now, or will use you very soon, based on the daily choices you're making as you live out your Christian walk.

In portrait dreams, we're getting free heavenly appraisals on the condition of our hearts, our spiritual potency, our level of understanding and wisdom, and a host of other things. Portrait dreams often leave us feeling pretty good, or they might leave us with a sense of heaviness or conviction. Here's the great part about portrait dreams: they are given to us because God loves us too much to let us stay as we are. He uses portrait dreams to call us to greater heights. He also uses these dreams to commend us and confirm we are on the right path. They suggest that more exciting adventures of faith and victory await us as we continue our walk with Him.

Prophetic Dream

Prophetic dreams are about the future. When God gives us these dreams, He is giving us a picture of events days, months, or sometimes years away. Prophetic dreams are given so we will pray and be prepared for what the Lord is showing us.

Any Christian can receive a prophetic dream, and I believe most of us will have at least a few of these throughout our lives. So, we all need to be familiar with them. Prophetic dreams can be about us, but they are often about others; thus, they are by nature, extrinsic dreams. An extrinsic dream is a dream about someone else. The dream might be about your spouse or a close friend, or even someone you've never met. By contrast, a dream in which you are the subject, is called an intrinsic dream. For most people, including myself, our dreams tend to be intrinsic. That is, God is showing us things about ourselves that will help us in our spiritual walk.

A great example of a prophetic dream can be found in Daniel 2:27–36. King Nebuchadnezzar is shown hundreds of years of world history in a single night. He sees the kingdoms that will arise long after his own has vanished. God's servant Daniel, a man with a powerful gift of dream interpretation, repeats the King's dream and then goes on to interpret it. Daniel shares:

> *You looked, O King, and there before you stood a large statue—an enormous, dazzling statue, awesome in appearance. The head of the statue was made of pure gold, its chest and arms of silver, its belly and thighs of bronze, its legs of iron, its feet partly of iron and partly of baked clay. While you were watching, a rock was cut out, but not by human hands. It struck the statue on its feet of iron and clay and smashed them. Then the iron, the clay, the bronze, the silver, and the gold were broken to pieces at the same time and became like chaff on a threshing floor in the summer. The wind swept them away without leaving a trace. But the rock that struck the statue became a huge mountain and filled the whole earth. This was the dream, and now we will interpret it to the king.*

Daniel goes on to interpret the dream and shows King Nebuchadnezzar that his dream is actually detailing the rise and fall of four great empires. One day, all world empires will be demolished before an unstoppable force—a rock (the Kingdom of God)—that will rule the earth forever and put an end to all man-made kingdoms.

I remember a particularly troublesome prophetic dream I had in May of 2016. As I fell asleep I observed a man of Middle Eastern descent standing before me. He was wearing a shirt with various Lego and Disney characters on it. I knew intuitively he was a terrorist made to look like an ordinary American citizen who blended into society. Across from him was another Middle Eastern man who I could only see from behind. I knew the man wearing the

Disney shirt took his orders or inspiration from this other man standing off to the side. I then saw a large world map where written in cursive over one of the continents was the word "Allegiance." Then I woke up.

I was greatly troubled in my spirit and felt the Lord was highlighting that another terrorist attack would soon occur, only this time not in New York City, but in Orlando, Florida. I believed the attack would occur at a Disney theme park so I immediately began to pray and intercede for the attack to be stopped or discovered right before it would happen. I'll never forget the morning of June 12, 2016 as I turned on the news to see blasted across the television screen "Terror attack in Orlando, FL, dozens killed."

I listened as the network described one of the worst mass shootings in U.S. history when a man of Middle Eastern descent opened fire killing 49 people. I fully expected the program to cut to a news anchor standing in front of a Disney theme park. To my surprise the attack occurred not at a theme park, but at a nightclub. I then thought to myself, *I guess I interpreted that part wrong. The shirt the man was wearing wasn't indicating an attack at a theme park, rather it indicated the city in which the attack would take place.*

However, I learned a few days later that before the gunman settled on attacking the nightclub, he had scouted several Disney theme parks and areas. For some reason at the last minute, he abandoned his plans to attack the parks and settled on a nightclub instead. This change of venue didn't lessen the horror of the attack, or its repulsiveness or evil. But can you imagine the added horror of reading about an attack where 49 five to ten year old children had been killed?

I believe many other Christians received prophetic warning dreams of this attack. I believe the prayers of God's people lessened the severity of the attack and turned it away from the elementary school aged children. Can I be certain of this? No, for those things pertain to God. But I know this. I've received a couple of other prophetic dreams where the images and scenarios I saw unfold in the dream never materialized. If the prayers of God's people avert even some of these horrible events or lessen the severity of others, then the intercessions offered to the Lord are worth our time and energy.

For most of us, the prophetic dreams we receive speak to issues of our own future or another's, calling us to intercede for them. We may sometimes receive prophetic dreams about our local church or city. The Lord may even give us a prophetic dream about our nation or a political leader because he is calling the church to pray for that individual.

Regardless of the sphere He chooses to reveal to us (personal, local, national, or international), it is still a high honor to be entrusted with revelation from the Lord pertaining to the future. When we receive this revelation, we should pray and be faithful with how we handle it. Many times the revelation is given, and we are not even supposed to share it with others, simply pray and prepare. There are times, however, when it is permissible for the individual to share it. In those times, we should be careful to do it with tact, humility, and in a spirit of prayer.

Healing Dream

The next type of dream we'll look at is especially powerful. For you see, my friend, a dream can sometimes bring more healing in twenty minutes than twenty years' worth of therapy. When God grants a healing dream He is literally repairing wounds so deep, that to even address them, He must do so while we're sleeping because our defenses are down. Rather than me explaining healing dreams to you, I want instead to tell you about a man who was healed from one.

Jonathan loved Melissa from the moment he laid eyes on her. She was a little young, but many couples marry young and make it, despite what the statistics say. Besides, Melissa shared a deep faith in God, as did Jonathan. People knew there was something special about this couple. God's hand of favor was on them both. Like any couple, they had dreams. Jonathan was good with his hands and was a master craftsman. He could build anything. Who knows, maybe one day he would build them both a house and custom make every cabinet, bed, and piece of furniture in it. Melissa would need a spacious house; she wanted a large family where the voices of little children would be a mainstay.

What The Bible Teaches About Dreams

Though they were in love and had the same passions as any couple, they kept themselves pure. They purposed in their heart that they would remain chaste until their wedding day, and Jonathan knew Melissa would never violate that vow. That is, until Jonathan heard a rumor. Word reached him that Melissa was pregnant. At first, he thought this was some kind of cruel joke, and to even approach her about it was beneath his dignity. He knew they both would not compromise their convictions, and there was no room in either of their hearts to love another. Something was pointed out to him, and perhaps he saw it for weeks himself but was in denial. Melissa seemed to be, ever so slightly, well, "showing."

For days he could not get the betrayal out of his mind. He tossed back and forth in his bed at night. She seemed distant to him, like there was something she wanted to say to him but never knew how to begin. Something had changed in their relationship, but it had been gradual. Finally, one night he asked her. "I've heard something horrible, and I don't want to believe it. Melissa, are you pregnant?" When she answered him, tears streaming silently down her cheeks, his heart stopped. "Yes," she replied.

It was true. He was in a fog. He couldn't remember all of the details of what she told him. She gave him the wildest excuse ever conjured by a guilt-ridden mind. He would have none of it; no sane man would. He decided to break off their engagement quietly because even though crushed to the core, he still loved her and didn't want to make their break up big news around town. Better to just let people find out here and there, through quieter channels, he thought.

The night he broke off their engagement he couldn't sleep. He tossed and turned and remembered all the times they enjoyed together. The day they met. The day they declared their love for one another. The day she betrayed him, the day he realized she had been with another man. Finally, after what seemed like hours he drifted off to sleep.

He then had a most amazing dream. A dream that in one swift stroke explained everything—and healed everything.

When he awoke, Joseph sent for Mary, for he intended to marry her. The dream not only healed his broken heart, but it confirmed the prophecy Mary mentioned—the same one he could not believe. It was true, and now he knew it. The child she carried was not from man, but from God. From her womb would come the Savior. He would save His people from their sins.

I had to temporarily disguise that story because we often dismiss the emotional turmoil that transpired between those two verses of Matthew 1:18–19. However deep the hurt must have been for Joseph, God healed it all in a single night in one dream. Healing dreams are sent to help us work through the pains and disappointments life has thrown our way.

Sometimes, the Lord gives us a dream to show us a new perspective on something we are going through. Sometimes it is a simple revelation about the motivation behind another's cruel act toward us. Perhaps the Holy Spirit shows us why they hurt others— because they themselves are so deeply wounded. The insight allows us to heal and even pray for the one who wronged us. Some healing dreams help us heal from emotional pains rooted in our childhood. When God chooses to send a healing dream, we can be sure the balm of heaven, once applied, will require no repeat surgery. For God does all things well.

Spiritual Warfare Dream

Throughout our lives we will engage the enemy of our soul in an ongoing battle for our hearts and minds. The Lord will give us spiritual warfare dreams to highlight spiritual conflicts going on in our churches, communities, and within our own souls. Dark demonic forces will also give us spiritual warfare dreams from time to time which are meant to fill us with fear and dread. These dreams usually center on violent attacks where we witness images of attacking demons or wild predatory animals like bears, leopards, or swarms of wasps.

Oftentimes spiritual warfare dreams involve guns and other violent weapons where evil, shadowy figures are opening fire on us, attempting to snuff out our life. In the dreams we can learn much about the plans of the enemy by dissecting these warfare dreams and discovering what areas the enemy plans to mount an offensive against us. We can then shore up those areas to counter any coming attack. In this scenario the dream is akin to vital field intelligence where we receive advance notice regarding the troop movements and plans of the enemy.

Cleansing Dream

Cleansing dreams are another category of dream that you will have from time to time. These dreams highlight areas of our lives that need cleansing or detoxification due to ungodly influences or sin that have crept into our lives. The Holy Spirit uses cleansing dreams to highlight our need for repentance, cleansing, and spiritual restoration.

You'll know a cleansing dream when you get one because they typically involve imagery such as showering, taking your car through a drive through car wash, or, I hate to be crude here, but…cleansing dreams will often involve imagery related to relieving oneself in the bathroom. If you've ever had a dream scene involving public restrooms, toilets, or the like, then you've likely had a cleansing dream. The dream imagery of relieving oneself is a spiritual picture of the need to rid our bodies of toxins, carnal influences, and sin.

When God is trying to highlight these types of issues to us, then we'll often receive dreams of bathing, using the restroom, and even dreams of vomiting. All of these types of scenarios are in the same family of dream classification. If you dream of relieving yourself in public the dream is highlighting that some of the process you'll be going through will be "seen by others" or will not occur in isolation. This is a humbling dream but the end result is, that if we cooperate with God, we'll come out clean and prepared for greater service. Promotion comes when we rid ourselves of our "mess", and seek to be clean and holy as He is holy.

One final thought, sometimes God will give us a cleansing dream to rid us of a spiritual influence that has attached itself to us, without us engaging in any known sin. The dream is there to "flush" the issue or spirit off us as we sleep. In this case, the dream is simply a merciful act given to us by our loving Father who watches over us and cleans us as we sleep peacefully in His rest.

Revelatory Dream

Some of our dreams don't fall neatly into any of the nine dream categories we've mentioned thus far. These I label, "revelatory dreams." This is a nice designation because the core purpose of any spiritual dream is revelatory in nature. God gives us dreams to reveal things to us. To reveal our fears and heal them. To reveal warnings so we'll act on them. To reveal the future so we'll pray and intercede. Revelatory dreams cover a broad range of dream topics.

As we examined in chapter two, there were so many useful inventions and products that came to fruition from a dream. These dreams provided revelatory information concerning how to solve a current business problem or develop a new product. So, dreams related to creative breakthroughs and inventions can be categorized as revelatory dreams.

Finally, another common phenomenon are dreams in which the Lord provides a vision of a current event and shows us the spiritual significance behind it. He allows us to "peak behind the curtain" so we will properly understand what's really happening. Often, this would not be apparent without the Lord opening our spiritual eyes to view it from His perspective.

To Whom Does God Speak?

Now that we have covered the ten most common types of spiritual dreams, let us now consider some other truths about dreams. Two questions often raised when discussing spiritual dreams are: "What must we do for God to speak to us in a dream?" and "What kind of people does God speak to in dreams?" The answers I like to give are: nothing and everyone.

I know not everyone has had a spiritual dream, or so they think. I am actually convinced everyone has them from time to time. They've just gone unnoticed because, in our culture, we don't respect dreams, and we've been conditioned from birth to not pay them much attention. Sometimes it's a question of people saying they don't remember any of their dreams, spiritual or natural. All we have to do to begin receiving spiritual dreams is to start asking for them. I believe the Lord will grant that simple request. We'll discuss more about cultivating spiritual dreams in a later chapter.

To the second question, "What kind of people does God speak to in dreams,"? the answer is: everyone. Just as God sends rain on the just and unjust, so He speaks to all people through dreams, Christians and non-Christians. The majority of dreams we have recorded for us in scripture are of God's communications with His people. If we do an exhaustive study of dreams throughout the pages of the Bible, we'll also notice God speaks to unbelievers as well. The verses below illustrate this truth.

- God speaks to Abimelech about Abraham's wife (Genesis 20:1–6)
- God speaks to Laban as he pursues Jacob (Genesis 31:22–24)
- God speaks to a Midianite about their coming judgment (Judges 7:9–15)
- God speaks to Pontius Pilate's wife about Jesus' innocence (Matthew 27:19)

Dream Evangelism

When God speaks to an unbeliever through a spiritual dream, it is a tailor-made opportunity for the people of God to minister to that person. As Christians we alone have God's Holy Spirit within us. We can seek the Lord for the meaning of that person's dream, and when the interpretation is given, a door to witness about the Lord Jesus is wide open.

Only two men in scripture are said to have had the "gift" of interpreting dreams, Joseph and Daniel. There were others in biblical times who had the gift, but these are the only two mentioned. Both Daniel and Joseph saw the value of using dreams to point people to God. Both of these servants of God used their interpretative gifts to do just that.

After King Nebuchadnezzar has his dream interpreted in the book of Daniel, he is ecstatic that God could speak so clearly through another human being. His spirit obviously bore witness to the interpretation, and he knew Daniel was not like the other wise men of his court. He was so impressed with Daniel's prophetic abilities that there, on the spot, he gave witness to God before his entire royal court saying, *"Surely your God is the God of gods and the Lord of kings and a revealer of mysteries, for you were able to reveal this mystery"* (Daniel 2:47).

Since Daniel was willing to steward his gift properly by staying humble and giving God the glory, the Lord promoted him into high levels of government service. Later another king of Babylon was so impressed with Daniel's administrative abilities and his moral character that he too made a royal decree. This time the decree was that everyone in the land must "fear and reverence the God of Daniel" (Daniel 6:26). Daniel's favor with these powerful rulers all started when he interpreted a difficult dream. The gift was simply used to gain access. Once inside, it was Daniel's godly character that made him stand out amidst all the other pagan advisors the king had assembled around him.

Even today, spiritual dreams win people to Christ. I know of groups who go out in the streets during large venues, such as concerts or summer festivals, in major U.S. cities, and they offer dream interpretations from a Christian perspective. I think this is a wonderful opportunity to get the gift outside of the four walls of the church.

One of best at using dream interpretation as an evangelistic tool is Cindy McGill. Cindy has a powerful dream interpretation gift and she once shared with me how she and her husband Tim use the gift with people out on the streets. Lives have been powerfully touched and many have come into the Kingdom when this precious sister has introduced these seekers to "the revealer of mysteries." For those who feel called to a ministry of dream interpretation, it is my hope you will use this gift, not just for the people of God, but for a lost and dying world that desperately needs to hear a word from God.

Frequency of Spiritual Dreams

An important point I don't want us to miss is that there is no correlation between the number of spiritual dreams a person receives and that person's spiritual maturity. I have friends who are deeply committed Christians, some of whom are pastors, and they tell me they've never had a spiritual dream. I know other deeply spiritual people with an equally vibrant walk with God and yet they receive spiritual dreams all the time. Some people receive them frequently, but whether you receive spiritual dreams never, occasionally, or all of the time, it's no reflection on your walk with God.

I personally believe God speaks to every Christian in dreams from time to time, so I have a hard time believing that someone reports they've "never" had a spiritual dream. It's my opinion that they likely have experienced them, they just didn't recognize it as such. Or, if you have not respected dreams, you will rarely remember them, but be assured you've had them nonetheless.

Spiritual dreams ebb and flow in my own life. I'll go through seasons where I get them quite regularly. In other seasons, I'll have only a handful in any given year. Don't feel bad at all if you've not had a lot of spiritual dreams. If you ask the Lord to speak to you in dreams, and if you'll commit to obeying what He shows you in your dreams, then get ready. You'll start getting them more frequently. Our Father loves to give gifts to His children, especially to the children who love His gifts and will use them.

Maintaining a Balanced Perspective About Dreams

Dreams and dream revelation should have a place of respect in every Christian's arsenal of spiritual tools. There is no doubt they are both useful and inspirational in our lives. A word of caution is in order here. We should not seek to elevate dreams above their appointed function.

Throughout the pages of the Bible dreams are portrayed as special revelations God will use from time to time when speaking to us about important matters, but dreams are never portrayed to be the primary way God speaks to people. As a matter of fact, some of the best known dreamers in scripture have only a few dreams credited to them. How many dreams does the Bible record Daniel having? Three. How many for Joseph? Two. How many for Israel's greatest prophets like Isaiah, Jeremiah, or Ezekiel? None.

Now that is not to say that these men didn't receive dreams on an occasional or even semi-regular basis. I believe they likely did, but I just want us to be aware that the Bible does not elevate dream revelation into some kind of exalted status. My dear friend, you know how much I respect dreams. In my own life, they've been a rich source of inspiration, encouragement, and revelation. In comparison to all the other ways God has spoken to me over the years, dreams played a modest role, but when God *has* given them, they've been powerful in my life.

Because dreams can be mystical and mysterious, some people have an almost unhealthy attraction to them. Some Christians want to depend on dreams for everything. It's as if they are constantly asking God to send them a dream, so they'll know who they are to marry, where they are to live, when they are to have their next yard sale, and on and on.

The fact of the matter is that we have a perfect, infallible source of wisdom lying in front of us. That infallible source is God's word, the Bible, and the great thing is it's not written in complex layers of code and symbolism (well, for the most part)!

So, let us have the attitude that dreams are a unique and wonderful way God will sometimes speak to His people. We must be open to them, and certainly learning how to better interpret them is a smart endeavor that will bear much spiritual fruit in our lives. Let us also remember that our interest in dreams should never overshadow our interest in studying God's word. Nor should it overshadow our desire and willingness to hear our Father speak to us through teaching, preaching, prophetic words, and all of the other avenues we surveyed together.

Chapter 4

Why God Speaks in Mysteries and Symbols

Levels of Symbolism in Spiritual Dreams

WE NOTICE WHEN STUDYING scripture that dreams can vary greatly in the depth of symbolism appearing in each one. Some dreams are straightforward and the meaning is obvious. Other dreams are deeply symbolic where the meaning is difficult to ascertain. For the sake of study, let's further classify dreams by the level of symbolism they contain.

Our three categories are:

1. **Uncoded dreams**—dreams containing no hidden symbols and for which the meaning is immediately clear to the dreamer. Examples: Genesis 20:1–7, 1 Kings 3:5–15
2. **Simple coded dreams**—dreams containing simple, basic symbols, which upon reflection, can be partially decoded by the dreamer. Examples: Genesis 37:5–8; 9–10
3. **Complex coded dreams**—dreams containing deeply cryptic symbols, which upon reflection, are difficult for the dreamer to decode. Examples: Daniel 2:29–36; 4:10–18

Uncoded Dreams

Ah, if all dreams could be uncoded dreams! The reality is most of our dreams are simple coded or complex coded dreams. Uncoded dreams are those in which the message of the dream is crystal clear. In these dreams, usually one sees a written message pointing the dreamer to the action they are to take or to the truth they are to grasp. At other times they hear a voice that clearly tells them what to do.

Because of the symbolic nature of dreams and the difficulty we have extracting their meaning, I often hear people complain. They say things like, "Why won't God just speak to us clearly without all these symbols!" I simply must digress for a moment and share a story in which God did just that.

A woman once came to me and was upset about a situation she had been praying about for some time. It involved a member of her family who had a great financial need no one could meet. Her family member needed a significant amount of money to undergo an important medical procedure. She also needed a large sum of money to do some much-needed home repairs, but the finances were just not there.

The woman who had the dream told me she had been praying for a while but was not hearing anything from the Lord. She was frustrated and then said, "I don't know if God will provide her with the money or not. I'm not hearing anything." Later that night, still frustrated, she told the Lord, "I wish You would just speak to me in plain black and white!" That night she had a dream in which she saw a large billboard in the sky, like the kind erected all along the highways. The billboard was completely white except for a large message in black block letters which read: A FERVENT AND COMPLETE GODSEND.

She came to me later that week and told me she felt bad about getting frustrated and making that declaration to the Lord. She then told me about the dream she received, and that she felt God gave her a definitive, clear answer. I could only chuckle and agree. I told her, "Well, you wanted it in black and white. You got it in black and white. Yes, God is saying He will deliver to this woman a heavenly godsend. Financial provision to meet this need is coming. God has decreed it." God in His mercy looked past her frustration and answered her request just as she had asked Him to, in plain black and white.

Just a few weeks later, the family member she was praying for received a check in the mail for $10,000 from someone she knew who lived in another state. The note explained that they just felt led by God to provide this love gift and to use it in any way she wished. A couple of weeks after, the family member received a second check in the mail for several thousand dollars from a second person who also said they too felt led by God to send her money. Again, just as the prophetic dream had foretold a few weeks before, God had indeed released a godsend into this woman's life.

Simple Coded Dreams

A great example of a simple coded dream can be found in Genesis 37:5–8. This is the first prophetic dream Joseph had about his future as a high level government official. Let's see how Joseph describes it:

> *Joseph had a dream, and when he told it to his brothers, they hated him all the more. He said to them, "Listen to this dream I had. We were binding sheaves of grain out in the field when suddenly my sheaf rose and stood upright, while your sheaves gathered around mine and bowed down to it." His brothers said to him, "Do you intend to reign over us?" And they hated him all the more because of his dream and what he had said.*

Even his thick-headed brothers knew what this dream meant. In some dreams the coding is so light and transparent that its meaning is pretty obvious. Many of our dreams are the same way. Upon waking we get a general sense of what the dream means. Some of the dream's imagery is very clear with only a few parts requiring additional meditation.

I remember a simple coded dream once told to me where the message of the dream was a mild rebuke. The Lord was telling the person to quit putting their hopes in man to meet their financial needs. The dream had several scenes in it, each one reinforcing that concept. The person had a general sense of what the dream meant but there was just one part they couldn't understand. This individual told me, "It's the weirdest thing. In one part of my dream, I was digging around in the dirt, and I uncovered a statue of a cow. This cow was decorated in beautiful jewels and gold trimmings. What in the world does that mean?"

I told the person. "It's your 'cash cow'; you're still hoping to unearth a get rich quick scheme, but it's not going to happen. The situation you are in is only solved by allowing God to take control of your finances."

Complex Coded Dreams

These dreams are the ones that leave us scratching our heads. These are the very cryptic dreams full of deep symbolism. These are the dreams that, upon waking, you think to yourself, "What in the world was this crazy dream I had!" These are the dreams that require much prayer and reflection in order to understand the dream's message.

I remember a complex coded dream I interpreted a few years ago. A woman dreamed that she and her whole church were taking a trip on an airplane. Upon arrival at the airport, the woman noticed she didn't have her ticket or any money. She was told she could go to a kiosk and retrieve her ticket there.

When she attempted to print out her itinerary, a food menu came out instead. She was then told she was at the wrong kiosk and was directed to another—this one being a kiosk covered in vines that was located in a wooded, forest-like part of the building. She was never able to access her ticket, so a friend ended up purchasing another one for her. She then attempted to get something to eat, but she had no money. Another person stepped up and paid for her lunch. After all of this, she then prepared to board the plane with her original group.

I was very stumped at first, but the Lord eventually revealed the dream to me. Without getting into all of the details, the primary message of the dream was that the woman needed to take charge and become more prepared in life, spiritually and vocationally. Others had always been there to cover for her, but that luxury was not going to be there to the same extent that it had been in the past. It was time to become more intentional about her preparation for the things the Lord desired to do *in* her and *through* her.

Once she heard the interpretation, she verified its accuracy with the current state of her life; in fact, God had been speaking to her about these exact issues. I was able to share that the dream was granted in order to give her the emotional impetus to act on what she already knew in her heart needed to be done.

Complex coded dreams are not only full of rich symbolism, but they can often contain multiple scenes, some related to one another and others that appear disjointed. The steps we will go over later will aid you greatly in decoding these dreams. Now that we've briefly discussed the varying levels of symbolism contained in dreams, let's now consider why revelation is wrapped in symbolism in the first place.

The Hidden Nature of Revelation

There is one question that inevitably arises from anyone who studies dreams or has had their fair share of them. That question is, "What's with all these riddles and symbols. Why doesn't God just speak plainly to us?" I cannot think of a more natural or valid question. That question certainly crossed my mind many years ago. After much prayer and wrestling, I came to understand a little more clearly just why the Lord "hides" His revelation.

There is no quick answer to this question. God has several purposes for choosing to reveal Himself this way. I believe if we'll take the time to think these issues through we'll better understand why He works this way, and we may even come to appreciate it.

Revelation is Veiled Due to the Fall

There was only one man on the earth who enjoyed clear, unencumbered communication with God, and that man has been dead for close to 5,000 years. That man was Adam. Adam enjoyed the rare privilege of immediate access and intimacy with God because he possessed something the rest of us have never had—a completely sin-free nature. In those days before the fall Adam and God walked together in the cool of the garden, speaking of things both common and divine.

The primary reason we have interference in our communication with God today is because of sin, both present and generational. That sin creates a barrier between us and God and does not allow for the highest levels of clarity and intimacy in communication. The very fact that we do not speak to God as Adam did, is a symbolic picture reminding us that the catastrophic effects of the fall have not yet been fully reconciled. Some might say, "But Bryan, we've been redeemed by the Lamb. You're discounting what Christ did for us on the cross. We're covered by the blood, we're sons of God now!"

I will be the first to say, "Amen" and "Hallelujah" to that. We are cleansed by the blood of Jesus and made joint heirs with Christ. Through God's process of sanctification, we are being conformed (a present work, not a finished act) to the image of Christ (Philippians 1:6). The reality is, while one part of us craves the things of the Spirit, we still have an innate carnal nature that pulls us toward sin and rebellion. The word of God attests to this duel reality. We, as the redeemed, enjoy a measure of fellowship with God while still remaining works in progress who still struggle with the effects of the fall.

> *But if we walk in the light as he is in the light, we have fellowship with one another, and the blood of Jesus, his Son, purifies us from all sin. If we claim to be without sin we deceive ourselves and the truth is not in us.* 1 John 1:7–8

> *For in my inner being I delight in God's law; but I see another law at work in the members of my body, waging war against the law of my mind and making me a prisoner of the law of sin at work within my members. What a wretched man I am! Who will rescue me from this body of death? Thanks be to God—through Jesus Christ our Lord! So then, I myself in my mind am a slave to God's law, but in the sinful nature a slave to the law of sin.*
> Romans 7:22–25

Admittedly this is a paradox, but it is true nonetheless. The effects of sin still hamper our communication with God. One day we will be made sinless and perfect before God. At that time, we'll have restored to us all of the privileges that Adam enjoyed for a season. One of those benefits being direct communication with a Holy God. Until that day arrives, get used to the symbols, to the still, small voice sometimes hard to hear, to the ambiguity of it all.

Revelation is Progressive by Design

Another reason our communication with God is mysterious and incomplete is because God releases revelation based on relationship. The mind and ways of God are extremely deep. It takes both time and a growing relationship before we can even handle all that God wishes to reveal to us. Isaiah 55:9 reminds us, *"As the heavens are higher than the earth, so are my ways higher than your ways and my thoughts higher than your thoughts."*

We simply could not understand the mind of God in the first place were He to reveal it all to us in clear communications. We gradually understand more and more of the heart and mind of God as He slowly reveals Himself to us, through the Word, in a dream, or in that still small voice. When we are given a little touch of revelation in a dream, it is often only one aspect of a major truth or issue. Even with such minor revelations, He must still break it down into meaningful parts which we can understand. He often chooses to reveal these little parts in word stories, pictures, and symbols which enable Him to teach us profound truths using simple communicative devices.

We need to also understand that God does not cast His pearls before swine. God will not increase intimacy with someone who does not want it or treasure it. What is the single most telling aspect of the true level of intimacy between two people? Their level of communication and the "access" rights they have to one another. So in that respect it is helpful for us to think about how revelation and self-disclosure is treated in our own human relationships.

Before I met my wife I dated a few of the women that I knew in high school and college. On my first date with the person I didn't immediately tell them the intimate details of my childhood or my present life. No, first dates are good for small talk. Where you from? How many siblings do you have? What are your future career plans? Things like that make for good dinner conversation while you're getting to know the other person.

Now if there is a connection and an appreciation for that person you'll tell (reveal) a little more on date two, a little more on date three, and so on. The principle is this: as relationships grow over time in terms of love, respect, and trust, both parties will naturally increase their level of self-disclosure. No one spills their guts and reveals their most intimate selves on their first date, at least they shouldn't.

Now for the flip-side of this analogy. I've been married for over 15 years and my wife is my best friend. Pauline knows everything about me. She knows things about me that no one else on earth knows. She knows my hopes and dreams. She knows what makes me laugh and she knows what breaks my heart. She knows all the things about me that are honorable and good. She knows my deepest secrets, my failures, and my greatest fears.

I didn't reveal these things to Pauline on our third date. No, I gradually revealed more and more of myself to her because, as we grew in trust and intimacy, it was just the natural thing to do. I knew I could trust her with all of me and that she'd never use that revelation to harm me, only to help me. This is how God operates in his relationships as well. As we move closer to the Lord, we will naturally grow in our intimacy with Him and in our ability to hear

His voice. As we move closer to Him, He will soften the symbols, lessen the cryptic nature of revelations, and begin to self-disclose more clearly.

In Numbers 12:6–8 this biblical truth is clearly demonstrated, and, ironically enough, the very context is biblical revelation through dreams and visions. The Bible says:

> *When a prophet of the Lord is among you, I reveal myself to him in visions, I speak to him in dreams. But this is not true of my servant Moses; he is faithful in all my house. With him I speak face to face, clearly and not in riddles; he sees the form of the Lord.*

Because the depth of the relationship with Moses was so deep, at some point God quit with the burning bushes and began speaking to Moses as one man speaks to another man. The riddles and the dreams stopped. Moses was so close to God that he actually received a glimpse of what Adam used to enjoy, one-on-one, clear communication between God and His choice servant.

Revelation is Hidden so It Will Be Sought

Another reason God wraps revelation in symbols and parables is because He knows that we best learn truth we have had to work for or have experienced ourselves. When we spend time seeking God and laboring over a dream's meaning, we eventually get the revelation of that dream, and the "a ha!" that follows is a powerful teachable moment.

For example, what do you think is the best way to teach a new Christian about tithing? One strategy is to simply point out the many verses in scripture that teach the principle of sowing and reaping. Or you might sit the new believer down and explain the finer theological points of Malachi chapter 3. After all is said and done, there will still be a reluctance on the part of many to begin tithing.

Why? Because no one enjoys giving their hard earned money away, even if it's to God. If you doubt me, just look up the many studies completed that reveal the percentage of Christians actually tithing a tenth of their income to the work of the Lord. The results will astound you. We are, by nature, selfish little creatures, and even in the area of tithing we have to learn to let go and trust God. We have to learn that He really can do more with 90 percent of what He manages than 100 percent of what we can.

What if we sat a new convert down and told him something like this, "I showed you from the Bible that God calls us to be generous givers and to give to our local church, but I realize that it's hard to let go of your money. So, I have a proposition for you. I want you to not tithe for the next six months. Keep every last penny to yourself and do what you want with your paycheck each week. Then I want you to tithe at least 10 percent of whatever you make for the next six months. Don't miss a single tithe and when you present it each week I want you to say a little prayer thanking God for the ability to even earn a living and asking Him to bless you financially as you trust Him with the first fruits of your earnings each week."

After the end of that year, do you think the new convert would be a lifelong tither or a Christian who gives 1.5 percent of his income to God's work each year? I think we all know what the answer is. They would be a tither because they would have *discovered for themselves* that it leads to blessings. I have never met anyone who told me they trusted God with their finances, but He let them down. As a matter of fact, there is only one area in scripture where we are allowed to test God—and that is in our finances (Malachi 3:10). Just as a tither learns best by working through an experience, dreamers learn best when they must personally wrestle a bit, or work through, to decipher a dream's meaning.

When God calls a reluctant missionary, what do you think makes a greater impact? To send a dream with a clear message like, "Thus saith the Lord, You are full of fear about becoming a foreign missionary. Don't be afraid." Or, do you think it might provide a stronger emotional impact to wrap that message in a cryptic dream that requires the dreamer to search out the meaning?

A dream, for instance, in which the person sees a particular village of people walking, single file, off a cliff into a dark abyss. These downtrodden people are chained together with long chords separating each person. Every so often one of the villagers looks up, hoping to be rescued before it's their time to approach the cliff and plummet to their death. A great distance away, out of their line of sight, lays a golden key, lodged in a bright green bush.

The dreamer wakes up from her dream visibly moved and eager to understand its meaning. After weeks of prayer and searching, she decodes the dream and realizes that God is saying, "I've called you to this nation. Go and I will give you a key to these chains that will set these people free. In doing this you will fulfill the calling I've had on your life since you were a little girl." That's just another reason for those pesky little symbolic dreams we've had to labor to understand. When we finally "get it" we've often grown significantly in the process. God really does know what He's doing.

Revelation is Incomplete Because It Requires a Community

For you Lone Ranger types with the "It's me and God. I don't need anybody else" attitude, excuse me for a moment while I offend you and your theology. Another pattern we observe in learning the ways of God is a little truth I like to call, "The Principle of Interdependency."

Simply stated, God has set up a Kingdom, a church, yea an entire world, built on interdependency. Think about it. The earth was designed in such a way that no one single nation would have all the resources they required. That's why the Middle East is floating on oil. Large parts of Africa rest on abundant gold and diamond mines. North America has fertile plains that produce enough food to feed 300 million people while still having excess to export all over the world. God set up a world that would require give-and-take among nations because no single nation received all of His blessings. Even Israel had to trade with her neighbors.

In the church, there is no superstar Christian who is an expert administrator, intercessor, powerful teacher, highly skilled prophet, and apostolic minister who moves in miracles, interprets dreams, writes amazing hymns, and is an effective pastor at a local church. That person doesn't exist and never will.

So it is, even with something like God's communication with His church. Have you ever noticed how interdependent that can be? Think of some of the most powerful truths God has ever revealed to you. How did you receive that revelation? Chances are God taught you that truth through a teaching or sermon (another person), a prophetic word (another person), or perhaps from an interpretation of a dream (yet again, another person involved). Of course, I realize God often teaches us truths directly, but I still believe there have been times in all our lives when God chose to use another vessel in our spiritual growth.

In summary, one reason dreams are mysterious and hard to understand is because they force us to seek help from others in the body of Christ. Thus, dreams reinforce the lesson that we need each other and that, collectively, we make up "the body of Christ." Each of us brings something of value to the table as we all serve God together.

Chapter 5

Natural Dreams, Spiritual Dreams, Dark Dreams

Sleep Cycles

AMERICAN RESEARCHERS MADE A breakout discovery in the early 1950s. Physiologists and doctors confirmed that the human body has two distinct modes of sleep. These two modes are REM sleep and NREM sleep. REM (rapid eye movement) sleep was so named after an observation during particular sleep cycles where the subject's eyes could be seen darting rapidly back and forth. These movements mirrored the eye movements of patients who were awake. The eye movements are noticeably lessened during NREM (non rapid eye movement) sleep.

Further research revealed during a typical night's sleep, a person moves in and out of alternating periods of REM and NREM sleep. Gradually, as a person falls into a deeper and deeper sleep, he or she will enter the first cycle of REM sleep. After the first cycle completes, the person will move back into NREM sleep. This cyclical pattern continues throughout the night with the average person experiencing 4 or 5 REM cycles. REM cycles tend to get longer as the night goes on. The first REM cycle can be as brief as ten minutes, while the final one can last as long as an hour.[16] It is during REM sleep that most dreaming occurs. REM sleep makes up about 25 percent of our total sleep time each night.

As clinicians continued studying the sleeping habits of research subjects, they discovered that the human brain never shuts off completely, even during sleep. As we lay asleep in our beds each night, the brain rests but is not idle. When researchers attach sensitive monitoring equipment to people during sleep, they consistently see a buzz of activity, not only in the brain, but in the heart rate, breathing rate, and muscle tone of patients. All of this increases dramatically during REM sleep when the body reacts to dreams. Remember, while in a dream, one cannot distinguish the dream from reality.

Natural Dreams

Our brain at rest performs a function very similar to a computer being defragged. Only when we sleep does the mind take time to review the events of the day, process the images and people it saw, erase the junk, and then make judgments about it all.

With this understanding in mind, we observe what the ancients already knew: not all dreams have spiritual significance or are heavenly messages from God. Ecclesiastes 5:3 rightly observes, *"As a dream comes when there are many cares, so the speech of a fool when there are many words."* Most of the dreams we have are called, "natural dreams." These are dreams that occur as a natural function of the human brain at rest.

Natural Dreams Come from What We Have Seen, Heard, or Thought About

Each night as we rest, our subconscious mind reviews the day's events. These include the people we visited, the programs and commercials we saw on television that day, or the squirrel we saw outside our window that morning. Many times, the subconscious mind has not finished reviewing the events from the prior day or from several days before.

As our mind processes all of this information, it ends up here and there as little dream fragments or "dream snippets," as I like to call them. These are short dreams that incorporate some image, theme, or issue you've recently had on your mind. Some you are aware of, and some may be just below your recognition, originating solely in your subconscious mind. Most of the time natural dreams are not that valuable, and we should not spend much time being concerned with them, but there are exceptions.

As a diehard science fiction fan and a lover of film, I have to view one of my favorite movies, *Star Wars*, at least once every year or two. Otherwise, I'd be forced to relinquish my official geek badge, and I'm just not willing to do that. After viewing such a movie, it is not uncommon for me to see a brief appearance of an Ugnaught or a Stormtrooper in one of my dreams that night. Upon waking, I don't waste precious time praying and asking God to reveal the deeper meaning behind that image. I know a droid or some other character appeared in the dream simply because my mind was still processing the images I viewed that day. We need to know that our media intake, recent conversations, or things we've pondered lately will show up in our dreams. Such dreams are simply natural dreams and there is no need for us to decode these dreams or to be too concerned with them.

Natural Dreams Come from What We Have Ingested in our Body

It is well documented that certain medications create strange dreams. I've heard people tell me that there are particular kinds of cold medicines they cannot take because of the disturbing nightmares they get afterward. This is simply a case of a particular medicinal compound not agreeing very well with the body chemistry of that person.

Consuming excessive alcohol or other substances causes chemical processes to occur in the body which affect dreaming. Therefore, anytime someone ingests certain foods, drinks, or medicines, their brain may produce particular dream patterns related to the chemical activity going on in their body. These are the classic "pizza dreams" we hear about. These dreams might manifest as nightmares or just as really bizarre, nonsensical dreams with no relevance to the dreamer's life.

Natural Dreams Come from our Soulish Desires and Judgments

If we have conflict with another person who we feel treated us poorly or unjustly, then we'll often have a negative dream about that person. Sometimes, folks mistake these for spiritual dreams. They will then unfairly use the dream to say things like, "I know that person is not in God's will. God showed me something very negative about them." Many times, however, these types of dreams are not spiritual dreams; they're simply subconscious expressions of our dislike of that person. I always caution people to avoid quickly labeling a negative dream about someone as a dream from God. Many times, it is just our hurts speaking.

We should also realize that our soulish desires very commonly manifest in our dreams. Have you always desired to be a world famous musician? If so, it would not be uncommon for you to occasionally dream of yourself on stage performing before thousands of adoring fans.

Do you have a crush on your new co-worker? Do you find yourself making sure your paths will cross throughout the course of your day? Then it would be very common to dream of him or her. Perhaps in one dream you're walking along a path hand in hand, engrossed in one another's company. In another dream you're locked in a passionate embrace. Upon waking there is no need to go looking for some deeper meaning in the dream. It's a natural dream that originated from the desires of your own soul.

Natural Dreams Come from Unresolved Issues in our Life

Our subconscious mind will also attempt to get our attention about issues in our life that cause us stress or pain. Many times these are issues we have not wanted to deal with, yet our mind is alerting us to the fact that we need to. These issues can manifest as uncoded dreams or they can appear as complex coded dreams buried beneath layers of symbolism.

Our mind buries these messages in deep symbols because they are too offensive to us to be revealed openly. God has ordained this role for our subconscious mind as a way of revealing truths to us that we need to act on. We should not take the position that only spiritual dreams have value and we should completely ignore natural dreams. Again, most of the time, natural dreams are simply an outgrowth of the mind at rest, and there is no deep message attached to them—nor should we go looking for one. That being said, God will still use natural dreams, so we need to at least be open to the possibility.

Spiritual Dreams

Spiritual dreams are those dreams that come directly from God. They are divine communications sent to us in order to deliver a specific message God wants us to act on. The key question before us now is, "How do we tell the difference between a natural dream and a spiritual dream sent by God?"

The truth is it can sometimes be difficult to discern the two. There is no simple formula anyone can provide. We must apply the same "tests" to dreams that we would to any other form of revelation, especially when trying to discern its source. Ultimately there is no substitute for a personal, growing relationship with the Lord Jesus Christ. As we walk with Him daily, and as we stay grounded in the Word of God, we have our senses trained to discern what is from the Spirit versus what is from man (Hebrews 5:14).

With that being said, I would still like to share some general truths about spiritual dreams. These will prove useful tools to you as you weigh in your own heart and mind any dream you've recently experienced.

Spiritual Dreams Affect Us Emotionally

Spiritual dreams often move us emotionally, and upon waking, we get a definite sense that it was no typical dream. We get an intuitive sense that this dream had some sort of message we are supposed to seek God about. Granted, this is all very subjective, but I believe we can all attest to the occasional dream that moved us like a normal dream rarely does.

King Nebuchadnezzar told Daniel his dream "terrified" him (Daniel 4:5). In Genesis 41:8 it was reported that after awaking from the dream of the seven cattle Pharaoh's "mind was troubled." Joseph's dream of the sheaves of grain in Genesis 37 greatly excited him. These men were all moved emotionally by the dreams they had.

The key for this indicator is the strength of the emotion experienced, not whether it is positive or negative. Spiritual dreams tend to move us greatly upon waking. It's not easy to dismiss them. As a quick side note, many people report that spiritual dreams tend to wake them up immediately after the dream's conclusion, even if it is in the middle of the night, whereas with natural dreams, people tend to wake up at their normal time.

Spiritual Dreams Often Contain Lots of Symbols

Another way to indicate whether or not a dream might be from the Lord is by examining the level of symbolism in it. Spiritual dreams often contain a lot of cryptic symbols that require reflection, prayer, and a bit of "wrestling" in order to discern their meaning. Some natural dreams contain high levels of symbolism as well, but as a general rule, natural dreams are more straightforward than spiritual dreams. Natural dreams often consist of basic scenes, like eating a meal with a family member, talking with friends at work, or engaging in routine day-to-day activities that reflect the normal interests of one's life.

Spiritual dreams are more likely to contain strange images, like seven fat cows devouring seven skinny cows, giant statues containing a variety of metallic colors, or people morphing into animals who then disappear when exposed to sunlight. You get my point. Spiritual dreams are famous for causing the dreamer to awake proclaiming, "Whoa, I just had the strangest dream! What could it mean?"

Spiritual Dreams Unfold Like Movies and Have an Objective

Spiritual dreams are typically unified stories, complete with a theme, a main character or characters, and a simple plot or scenario that unfolds from beginning to end. Natural dreams, on the other hand, are often short scenes or snippets that seem disjointed and don't really advance a single narrative from scene to scene.

A dream from the Lord is often like a short film or a biblical parable. The dreamer can clearly identify a connection between the dream scenes and the dream can be described in terms of a main thrust or action which is being portrayed. The dreamer will often see an issue, a scenario, or a person and the dream will portray a positive or a negative outcome for that issue, scenario, or person. The dreamer will then awake with a dream assignment such as: to intercede, to understand, or to heed the warning of that particular dream.

Spiritual dreams, therefore, have a call to action. There is always a reason the Lord gives the dream. Spiritual dreams are not random, disjointed scenes, that don't call the dreamer to do anything differently after they wake up. Spiritual dreams are given because there is an action or understanding the Lord wants the dreamer to walk away with after the dream ends.

Spiritual Dreams Draw Us to Self-Reflection

Spiritual dreams, by their nature, often reveal things to us about our own spiritual condition or how God is presently working in our lives. As such, upon waking, these dreams naturally lead us to introspection about how we live our lives. These dreams seem to invite us to think deeply about our recent decisions, judgments, or our thoughts about a matter.

Many times natural dreams can just be a string of silly or nonsensical scenes that don't seem to move us, nor do they seem to draw us to consider important issues on a serious level. Dreams that challenge our preconceived ideas, cause us to reopen an issue we thought was settled, or point out things about our life that need changing, are often dreams from the Lord.

Let us recall the vision the apostle Peter had in Acts 10:9–17 about the unclean animals appearing on a great sheet descending from heaven. In this vision, God was challenging a theological belief Peter held, which was no longer valid in light of the new covenant. After the strange trance was over, scripture records that Peter was left "wondering about the meaning of the vision." This is typical of spiritual dreams and visions—they cause us to search our souls.

Spiritual Dreams Lead Us to Conclusions That Line up with Scripture

Any dream we have, upon interpretation, that leads us to do something against the clear teaching of scripture is: a) either a faulty interpretation or, b) a dream that is not from God. Spiritual dreams that come from heaven draw us closer to God and always contain directives, revelations, or insights supported by the Word of God. Remember, true spiritual dream revelation is revelation from God, and God does not contradict Himself. He will not tell us to do one thing in scripture and then tell us to do something totally opposite in a dream.

Therefore, if someone has a dream about their spouse not understanding the deeper things of the Spirit, and the person says to me, "I believe God has shown me my spouse and I are not compatible spiritually. I believe the Lord is calling me to leave my spouse and marry another." My answer is: "No friend, the Lord is calling you to get out of deception because you are violating the clear teaching of scripture."

Dreams must be handled with wisdom and spiritual discernment, and that is why we must never make a major life or ministry change based solely on an unconfirmed dream. If you have a dream you believe to be of the Lord, then you should have no problem sharing that dream with your pastor, elder, or some other person in spiritual leadership at your church. If, after prayer and counsel, the dream is confirmed, then and only then, should you act on it.

If we ever have a dream in which we have even the slightest doubt as to its origin, it is better to err on the side of caution and subject that dream to a little more scrutiny. Spiritual dreams from the Lord should be able to pass a simple test of basic questions. Therefore, when evaluating a spiritual dream, consider these very relevant questions.

- Does this dream's central theme or message contradict scripture in any way? Is this dream asking me to believe or behave in a way that violates any known principle or command found in the Bible?
- Does this dream present some "new revelation" I can find no basis for in the established Word of God? If I accept this dream's premise, will I be moving into completely new theological territory? Will I be standing alone as the recipient and guardian of this "new truth"?
- Is this dream challenging me to live in such a way that the fruit of the Spirit (Galatians 5:22–23) is more evident and consistent in my life?

Consequently, it goes without saying that spiritual dreams will draw us into a closer walk with God. The fruit of a spiritual dream will be positive spiritual growth, a call for more maturity on our part, and a call to make us better stewards of all that God has given us. In short, spiritual dreams call us to be better disciples of the Lord Jesus Christ. Spiritual dreams drive us to live out a lifestyle exhibited by the fruit of the Spirit as described in Galatians 5:22–23. Thus, the message of spiritual dreams will call us to greater levels of: love, joy, peace, patience, kindness, goodness, faithfulness, gentleness, and self-control.

Dark Dreams

As we've come to expect, when God creates something beautiful, Satan is quick to want to counterfeit and corrupt it. He does the same things with dreams. I wish I didn't have to cover this issue, but we simply must be cognizant of the fact that some dreams are inspired by the enemy. While there is no direct verse in scripture that says, "Satan can influence dreams," just talk to the millions of people who've had a dark dream, or a demonic dream as they're sometimes called, and they'll assure us that he most certainly can. A passage in Jeremiah hints pretty strongly that he can as well; we'll look at that one in a moment.

If Satan can change the molecular structure of one object and turn it into another as he did with the sorcerer's staff (Exodus 7:10–12), if he can show Jesus all the kingdoms of the world in an instant (Luke 4:5), or if he can implant a thought in a person's mind causing them to speak it out (Matthew 16:22–23), then I don't think it's a tall order to send someone a dark dream.

Satan has many purposes for dark dreams. He sends them primarily to torment, confuse, and deceive. The forces of the dark kingdom can send dreams to both Christians and non-Christians. One thing we have to be careful about is too quickly assigning a dream's origin to Satan simply because the dream causes fear or is about a dark subject. These kinds of dreams can come from God as well. Remember our foundational verse for understanding spiritual dreams is Job 33:16 where we are told specifically that God will sometimes send someone a dream "to terrify them with warnings."

Daniel once had a spiritual dream that was so disturbing to him his hands and knees trembled (Daniel 10:10). I'm not sure where this idea originated, but I've heard it for years now. It goes something like this. Satan is dark. His messages are always negative and leave you full of fear. God's messages are always positive and leave you with feelings of joy and peace. While that seems logical on the surface, a quick scan of the Bible will prove that to be very inaccurate.

God is indeed a God of love, peace, and mercy. He's also a God of judgment and fire. Therefore, not all spiritual dreams will be about rainbows, puppy dogs, and themes that leave us with a sense of peace. Sometimes, God gives an ominous dream and we must be open to this fact. If not, we risk ascribing to Satan, something which is, in actuality, from God.

Dreams from the enemy are always dark or deceptive in some way. Many people report that dreams from the enemy come in darker, muted colors, or entirely in black and white. Dark dreams usually leave one with no hope, no way of escape, and amidst the depressing themes, there seems to be no positive aspect at all—no offer of redemption. Dreams from the Lord don't have that quality. Spiritual dreams can sometimes deal with very dark themes (spiritual warfare, the tactics of the enemy, divine judgment, etc.) but, in spiritual dreams, there is a redeeming message or some avenue of hope portrayed in the dream. God is a God of mercy, and even in harsh spiritual dreams, we see His divine attributes of grace, mercy, or love contained somewhere within.

Dark Dreams Sent to Torment or Harass

The enemy will sometimes send dreams simply to torment people and fill them with fear. It could be that the person has reoccurring nightmares about a very traumatic experience they went through. It could be that in their dreams, they relive a rape, a horrible scene from an abused childhood, or the terrible things they saw in their service to their country during a time of war or while on a special mission. Through the dream, the enemy longs for the individual to stay in bondage to that experience and never experience the freedom that Christ offers.

The enemy could send the dreams with accompanying subtle messages such as: "you're not worthy of anyone's love," "you deserved the past you grew up in," or "God can never forgive you for the things you supposedly had 'orders' to do." Just remember, the enemy lies and twists events in such a way to keep us bound, depressed, and ineffective in our service for God. If he can't get to us in our waking hours, he will sometimes try to do it through a dream.

For dreams such as this, it is important for the people of God to cover themselves with the blood of Christ and rebuke the power of the enemy over their own life or the life of the one they are ministering to. Through prayer, the stronghold of nightmares can be broken, and the person can be set totally free.

Let us also be aware that recurring nightmares of past traumatic events can also be natural dreams. In these cases, rebuking the devil does no good. These dreams are our subconscious mind's way of telling us we've not yet healed from these events. Oftentimes, God will use a skilled counselor to help people work through those issues in order to see freedom in their lives.

For some dark dreams, the word "torment" might be a little strong. Some experience dreams more on the level of demonic harassment. Perhaps they dream continually of God not meeting a real need in their life or of the people closest to them betraying them. The enemy could be trying to send confusion, paranoia, or plant seeds of distrust in the person's mind. Again, if a dream is discerned to be demonic in nature, then this is where the help of the body of Christ is vital.

Those with a strong anointing for discernment may need to be consulted, so when the saints pray together in unity, the plans of the enemy will be identified where they can then be canceled and broken through prayer. God has called us to be set free, and we do not have to settle for or believe the lies of the enemy, whether they come in our minds during our waking hours or during a dream when our defenses are down.

Dark Dreams Sent to Deceive

Lastly, there is another major purpose Satan has in mind when he sends a false dream: to deceive people. Since dreams are mystical, spiritual experiences that can leave the person feeling "special," he often sees the advantage of using a dream as the seedbed for the lies he wishes to implant. "Why it must be true, I had this amazing dream! God is speaking new revelation to me. I'm special. I'm the only one He has trusted with this revelation." When people start talking like that, I get nervous.

Some are unaware of the origins of Islam. It was started by a dream given to Muhammad. The message supposedly came from the angel Gabriel. We Christians know that what later came from these "new revelations" was the Koran and an entirely new religion. The message Muhammad received was not that the religion of the Old and New Testaments was wrong per se, *it was just incomplete.* In Islam, Moses, Abraham, and the prophets are honored, but Muhammad is elevated above them all. The key issue is that in Islam, Jesus is a prophet, not the eternal Son of God. How did millions of Muslims in the world come to believe this? Because a man long ago told them, "I had a dream from God. He's shown me a new, deeper revelation."

How many more off-shoot groups or Christian cults have been started throughout history due to some "revelation" revealed in a dream or vision claimed by some person? Many. We must remember that there is nothing new under the sun. Self-appointed prophets, false representatives of God, have been peddling their erroneous revelations for thousands of years. That is why the Bible warns us that of the many ways Satan seeks to deceive people, dreams are sometimes his method of choice. The prophet Jeremiah warns, *"Do not let the prophets and diviners among you deceive you. Do not listen to the dreams you encourage them to have. They are prophesying lies to you in my name. I have not sent them declares the Lord"* (Jeremiah 29:8b-9).

If we do not make the Bible the foundation and final jury on any message, angelic visitation, or dream that someone has, then we are headed for trouble and deception. It just can't be said any more clearly than the apostle Paul once taught when he cautioned the church:

> *I am astonished that you are so quickly deserting the one who called you by the grace of Christ and are turning to a different gospel—which is really no gospel at all. Evidently some people are throwing you into confusion and are trying to pervert the gospel of Christ. But even if we or an angel from heaven should preach a gospel other than the one we preached to you, let him be eternally condemned!*
> Galatians 1:6–9

A Final Thought

As we spend time examining our dreams and learning more about how they operate, we will grow more skilled in interpreting them and recognizing their origin. Don't worry if you cannot always tell the difference between a natural dream, a spiritual dream, or a dark dream. With time and practice it will become more and more clear, I assure you. Ask God to increase your discernment about dreams and He will. Take comfort in John 16:13 which promises us, *"But when he, the Spirit of Truth, comes, he will guide you into all truth."* Jesus promised us help in detecting truth, and, my friends, that includes dreams as well.

Chapter 6

Principles for Successful Dream Interpretation

LET'S NOW EXPLORE THE foundational issues related to successfully interpreting dreams. Over the years, I have discovered some basic principles that will help you grow exponentially in your ability to interpret your dreams. These principles will also enable you to help others who are seeking to understand their dreams.

Principle #1: Dream Interpretations Come from God

Though this statement is a given fact for some, still others, including some Christians, believe all that is required to interpret dreams is a single attendance at a local dream seminar. Of course, they feel they'll also need their handy, dog-eared copy of the latest dream symbol book, so one can look up the meaning of "tree," "dog," or "condominium." I could not disagree more strongly with this rote method.

It is true, there are two requirements for understanding any dream. These are the natural component and the spiritual component. The natural component incorporates all of the known understanding from the fields of psychology and oneirology. There is much good that comes from studying these research findings. The Christian world has produced its own pioneers in this field in men like Morton Kelsey and John Sanford.

Through studying these works, we become familiar with the nature of dreams, their penchant for symbolism, their propensity for layered meanings, and their value as a tool for self-reflection. I would never discount the importance of learning these truths and incorporating their use in our dream analysis. All truth is God's truth.

However, what I get uncomfortable with is when I see Christians leaning entirely on these mechanical, naturalistic rules to the exclusion of the spiritual component in dream interpretation. Let us be reminded of what Daniel declared to Nebuchadnezzar in Daniel 2:27–28, *"No wise man, enchanter, magician or diviner can explain to the king the mystery he has asked about, but there is a God in heaven who reveals mysteries."* Let us not forget another talented dream interpreter, Joseph, who when asked by Pharaoh for the meaning of a dream replied, *"I cannot do it . . . but God will give Pharaoh the answer he desires"* (Genesis 41:16).

The apostle Paul makes a powerful statement about these two aspects of truth that is applicable to our discussion of dreams. He explains in 1 Corinthians 2:10–14:

> *The Spirit searches all things, even the deep things of God. For who among men know the thoughts of a man, except the man's spirit within him? In the same way no one knows the thoughts of God except the Spirit of God. We have not received the spirit of the world but the Spirit who is from God, that we may understand what God has freely given us. This is what we speak, not in words taught us by human wisdom but words taught by the Spirit, expressing spiritual truths in spiritual words. The man without the Spirit does not accept the things that come from the Spirit of God, for they are foolishness to him, and he cannot accept them, because they are spiritually discerned.*

Therefore, I promise you that anyone who would attempt to interpret your dream relying solely on technical methods will not arrive at the complete meaning of that dream. Sure, I'll grant that some simple coded spiritual dreams can be interpreted using purely mechanical methods. However, without the enlightenment of the Spirit, an interpreter will not be able to discern the fuller, deeper meaning of our spiritual dreams.

Principle #2: Pray for the Interpretation of Your Dream

James 1:5 promises us that God will give wisdom to those who ask for it. When we receive a spiritual dream from the Lord, the first thing we should do, after writing it down of course, is to ask the Lord to help us decode its meaning. If we will take the time to pray and ponder over our dreams, I believe God will give us the interpretation for most of our dreams. It might take a few hours. In some cases, for really difficult dreams, it might take a few days or even a few weeks, but He will reveal the meaning to us. He gave us the dream because there is a message He wants to communicate. We must simply show Him that we are eager to receive it.

Principle #3: Examine Your Feelings and Emotions During the Dream

Immediately after you wake from your dream, you may have a sense of elation, wonderment, or peace. Or you may have a sense of conviction, heaviness, or even concern. Here is the good news: simply identifying the overall feelings and emotions the dream left with you decodes fifty percent of the dream's meaning.

How you felt during the dream overall, and especially during key parts, is a huge clue to the dream's interpretation. Warning dreams concern you. Healing dreams make you cry tears of joy. Calling dreams excite you. You might not immediately know what all the symbols mean, or even be close to identifying the predominant theme, but you'll already be able to answer the number one question: "Was this a *good* dream or a *bad* dream?"

We see this truth illustrated in scripture. In the second chapter of the book of Daniel, King Nebuchadnezzar has a dream that scared him so badly he did something unheard of. He could not chance that his wise men would simply invent some meaning, which even he might fall for. This dream shook him so much he devised a plan to ensure he got the proper interpretation. He told his wise men that not only did they have to interpret his dream, they also had to tell him what he dreamed the night before! He then followed up with a death threat. If they could not deliver on this critical request, they'd all be dead soon. God gave Nebuchadnezzar a prophetic dream that scared the daylights out of him.

In the 37th chapter of Genesis, Joseph has a calling dream that excites him so much he just can't keep it to himself. He tells it to his mother. He tells it to his father. He tells it to his eleven brothers. I'm sure he told it to the house servants and the local barn stall cleaner as well.

Dreams will have an emotional impact on us, good or bad, and that is a huge clue to the dream's meaning. However, sometimes we may have a dream and awake perplexed, unable to nail down any one emotion, positive or negative. Sometimes prophetic dreams leave us this way, though I've seen calling dreams, confirmation dreams, and just about every other type do this as well. Thankfully, this is usually not the norm. Most of the time we wake up with definite feelings about how the dream moved us.

In a dream we will be emotionally impacted not by just the characters we interact with, but also by animals or inanimate objects. If we are walking along a trail at night in the pitch black and all around us we hear the howling of wolves getting closer and closer, yet we feel no fear, that is a big clue. Shouldn't we normally feel fear? Why didn't we in the dream? The emotion we felt alerts us that the wolf scene means something; it moved us somehow, either negatively or positively.

Or perhaps in one dream we are invited into the home of a person we are considering going into business with, but the moment we walk into the person's house we feel uneasy, like there is a darkness in this house. Upon waking, that uneasy feeling associated with that person's house (i.e., that person or some aspect of that person) is a big clue to the dream's meaning. So, let us pay close attention to our emotions and feelings in our dreams. When I'm interpreting a dream, one of the first questions I ask the dreamer is, "What were you feeling during this dream? How did this dream move you as it unfolded?" The answers to these types of questions are interpretive gold.

Principle #4: Identify Your Place in the Dream

Another early step in interpreting a dream is to identify your position in the dream. Were you the key character in the dream? We're you involved in all the dream's scenes as an active participant? If the answer is "yes," then the dream is about you or some aspect of your life. If, on the other hand, you were not even in the dream, but rather served as an unseen spectator of the events unfolding before you, then this dream is more likely not about you. It's about the person or group of people portrayed in the dream. When we are the star of the show and are dreaming about ourselves that is called an intrinsic dream. A dream that is primarily about another person is called an extrinsic dream.

Most of the time, we dream about ourselves, so our dreams tend to be intrinsic. I've found, however, that intercessors and others with prophetic gifts tend to also get lots of extrinsic dreams. Perhaps it's because the nature of their gifting involves the need to have insights about others as they are praying for and ministering to them. God often chooses to deliver those insights through dreams.

There is one other issue we should address while we're on the topic of extrinsic dreams. When we receive a spiritual dream about someone else should we share it with that person? I personally do not share most of the dreams I have about others unless I feel a strong unction from the Lord to do so.

My reason for this is that if the dream is only providing some minor insight about common everyday issues, then what is the point of sharing something so insignificant? Is it really going to profit the person? The exception for me, however, are warning dreams. If I get a negative dream about someone regarding an issue that might affect their spiritual or physical safety, I will usually just spend some time in prayer for the person. If that time of prayer doesn't lift my burden and the dream lingers in my spirit for days, then I will usually share the dream with the person.

Principles For Successful Dream Interpretation

If I get a very positive dream about someone and I know the person is open to dreams, then sure, I'll share that as well. If I get a spiritual dream informing me of some negative trait in that person, I won't share. I assume God has given me that information so I'll pray for them. Do we really want to run around constantly telling people, "The Lord revealed to me last night that you really struggle with selfishness, but hey, I'm prayin' for ya!" If you begin a policy of sharing every single negative dream you have about others, then prepare to be a very lonely person who is never invited to any parties.

In summary, if you get a very positive dream about someone and think it will really lift their spirit, then yes, share it. If you get a negative dream about someone regarding sin in their life or some other negative issue, then just pray for the person as you would want them to do for you. If you get a warning dream about someone's safety don't put fear in their life by feeling you have to tell them. Just pray for them. If you feel led by the Lord to share the warning, then by all means share the dream, and begin a season of prayer for that person's protection.

Principle #5: Reduce the Dream to Its Simplest Form

Another common mistake we make in dream interpretation is when we are so focused on the dream's minor details that we miss the big picture. Some dreams, especially longer ones involving numerous scenes and characters, will have a lot of little details. Our natural instinct is to look for some hidden meaning in every single element in the dream. Usually this is neither necessary nor helpful.

No matter how complex the dream is, beneath it all is a single message crying to be heard. We need to view all of the symbols, items, and characters in a dream as set pieces merely there to help set the mood and reinforce the central message that the master playwright, God, purposes for the dream. Therefore, when initially reviewing the dream try hard to find a central theme or predominant message that will key you in to the dream's main point. This is in my opinion the most important step in dream interpretation. You simply must learn how to boil a dream down to a central plot or theme, and, if needed, allow for only two or three sub-plots. If you cannot learn to simplify the dream, you will have a very difficult time trying to capture the dream's meaning.

Let's suppose a man has a dream that his family has come into a nice inheritance. Let's say there are three brothers and their father informs them that each son will get $100,000. The oldest son enrolls in radiology school where a few years later he earns his degree and now makes a very nice annual income. The middle son uses his $100,000 to buy stock in a new product that makes vegetables taste like candy, but they still maintain the nutritional value of vegetables (hey it's a dream, a man can wish can't he?). After this invention, the middle son becomes a very wealthy millionaire and a hero to kids all over the world.

Let's say in the dream the youngest son uses his share to take all of his friends on a two-year cruise around the world where they will party non-stop in Miami, Rio de Janeiro, and other hot spots. After the cruise he comes back with $35,000 and spends it on a nice new jet ski.

Before the dream revealed the spending habits of the three brothers, let's pretend there was a little scene where the postman delivered the inheritance notification to the boy's father by saying, "Good morning, Bob. I have a letter for you." Let's also say that the middle brother's story included a scene where a kid approaches him and says, "Wow, I love your vegetables! Do you have chocolate-flavored eggplants?" The middle son replies, "No, but I have a raspberry-flavored eggplant. How's that sound?" "Oh yeah, I love raspberries!" Now to the point. Does the scene where the postman delivers the letter really play a major role in this dream? No.

The main theme we see in this dream is how two brothers used their inheritance (their God-given life opportunities) wisely, and how one brother foolishly squandered the resources God gave him. This is basically a spin-off of the parable of the talents as described in Matthew 25:14–30. What does the part about raspberry-flavored eggplants have to do with this dream's central message? Absolutely nothing.

I am not suggesting we discount all minor characters and events in any given dream. Sometimes those little details are the key to

Principles For Successful Dream Interpretation

interpreting the dream. I'm simply saying that once the overall message of the dream is decoded, don't worry if you can't make sense of every single little detail. Sometimes those abstract details are simply what I call "filler material." Think of them as heavenly MacGuffin devices used to get the plot rolling.

In chapter 10, "7 Dreams Decoded," you are going to get a chance to practice reading over some dreams where you will see many little details. You will have to make a judgment as to whether they are central to the dream's message or just filler material. Some details might even be helpful to the dreamer, but if they are not central to the dream's primary message you could still interpret the overall dream correctly. You would simply be missing some of the minor insights.

Before we go to the next principle I have a homework assignment for you. This will give you practice in the skill of reducing a complex narrative into its simplest form. I want you to pick five movies that you really like and force yourself to describe the plot of those movies in one sentence, and one sentence only. If you go over one sentence you owe me a Coke when we meet in person. I'll illustrate this principle by completing this assignment myself. Here goes:

E.T. – A friendly alien is accidentally left behind on earth and must befriend a little boy to help him return home.

The Lord of the Rings – An ancient evil being seeks a ring of great power to enslave his world, but a group of nine brave companions pledge their lives to destroy the ring before it can be used for evil.

How the Grinch Stole Christmas – A bitter old Grinch plans to steal all the Christmas presents from the children of Whoville until one little girl softens his heart causing the Grinch to relent as he learns the true meaning of Christmas.

The Silence of the Lambs – The FBI, with help from a brave, inexperienced female trainee, convinces a brilliant, imprisoned psychopath to help them catch a serial killer who is always one-step ahead of the law.

Signs – A minister who has lost his faith, finds it again, and just in time to save his family from a hostile alien force that has invaded the earth.

Principle #6: Dreams Are Cryptic and Symbolic

I know I'll win no dinner invitations from any of you for revealing something so obvious, but we must not overlook this. One of the biggest mistakes people make in interpreting their dreams is to interpret them too literally. A classic example is the common rape dream which many women report having. This is almost never a warning dream alerting someone that they are about to be raped. Remember, dreams are symbolic, so we have to get into that mindset when we think about them.

What is rape? What does it do to a woman's psyche? It's a horrible violation of her personal liberty and her trust in people. It's a violation of something very intimate in her life (her sexual self). It's a classic demonstration of a more powerful force imposing its will on someone unable to stop it. When a woman has a dream of being raped, it is often a picture of an extreme, unjust act committed against her. It can also portray a violent ripping apart of something very precious to that individual. Context will reveal the particulars but you get my point.

What about dreams where you see a friend or family member lying in a casket? Does that mean we are to immediately begin fasting and praying because God is showing us that Satan plans to kill them in the next 48 hours? No, usually it's not that at all. Of course, we have to use discernment and that is why Principle #1 is listed as Principle #1, "Dream Interpretations Come from God." God may certainly warn us of someone's future death, but we should not rush to that judgment.

In fact, I would suggest that all dreams of death, rape, carnage, or nuclear war are not to be taken literally unless the Holy Spirit tells you differently. Otherwise, always look for ways in which a dark symbol portrays some facet of the act, rather than prophesying the literal act in your life.

Metaphors in Dreams

Dreams are symbolic in more ways than just the images we see. They are often cryptic in the actual transmission of those images. Dream imagery can come to us in the form of metaphors, funny word pictures, and even in colloquialisms. Let's explore a few of these concepts in more detail.

This is, in my opinion, one of the most fascinating aspects of dreams and one of the reasons I love them so much. I am amazed at how often I see metaphorical devices showing up in my dreams and in the dreams of others. What's even more interesting is that sometimes the dreamer is not even familiar with the specific speech or literary device showing up in their dream, yet it's often key to the interpretation.

By definition a metaphor is a figure of speech where a word or phrase used to describe one thing is applied to another thing in order to highlight a comparison or similarity between those two things. A classic metaphor we all recognize would be, "Her speech is like music to my ears." The metaphor being that her words are so pleasant they bring joy to others just as music does. Another common metaphor would be, "Michael is a night owl." This metaphor uses a common animal known for its nocturnal activities to highlight that Michael likes to stay up late.

An essential "key" to interpreting dreams is to see an object, not just for what it is, but to see that object for what it is like or what it could creatively symbolize. Chapter 7 will illustrate this concept in more detail. When we start to think about objects metaphorically, then we are starting to become fluent in the language of dreams.

And finally, dream meanings sometimes come out of colloquial expressions or old sayings. I know a woman who once had a scene in her dream where she could not fit into a pair of jeans, no matter how hard she tried. A dream scene like that doesn't appear to have much meaning, and we'd be tempted to toss it out as irrelevant. Luckily this woman did not do that. God gave her insight, and she suddenly realized that part of the dream was Him telling her that she had "gotten too big for her britches!"

Idioms in Dreams

In addition to metaphors, idioms are common in dreams as well. Idioms are popular expressions that have a completely different meaning from the actual words making up the phrase or expression. Popular idioms in America would include: "He escaped by the skin of his teeth" (translation: he barely got away) or "He's over the hill" (translation: he's old).

Let's take a look at how an idiom might be hiding in a dream. Suppose a recent college graduate has job offers with two excellent companies and she is trying hard to determine God's direction. She has a powerful dream one night in which she dreams about the two companies. In one dream, she sees herself at Company A. She feels great. She's making new friends, and she's picking things up really quickly. The scene changes and now she sees herself walking the halls of Company B. In one scene she opens her desk drawer and finds a large, live salmon flapping around. In another scene she walks up to collect her employee ID badge but notices a dead trout lying next to some books over to her left side. Then she wakes up with a strong sense in her spirit that this dream is from the Lord but she has no idea how to make sense of the imagery.

What in the world does this dream mean? The Lord is indeed trying to tell her something, and He's using an old trick up His sleeve to deliver the message. He's using an idiom common to the young woman's culture. What's the idiom? He's telling her to accept the offer at Company A. She'll be well received there and will pick things up quickly. She'll be happier there. She needs to decline the offer from Company B. Why? Because if she goes there she'll be a "fish out of water."

So, another skill you need lots of practice with to become a good dream interpreter is to know the idioms of your particular culture because God often uses them in dreams. Here's another little exercise to sharpen this particular skill for future dreams you'll interpret. Take the following idioms and think of creative ways these phrases could be encoded in dream imagery. By practicing this skill of reverse engineering the encoding process, you will strengthen your ability to make sense of seemingly nonsensical dream imagery.

How might the following American idioms be encoded in dream form?

- Let the chips fall where they may   (let whatever is going to happen, just happen)

- Bite off more than you can chew   (getting involved in something beyond your abilities)

- Missed the boat   (missing an opportunity)

- Water under the bridge   (forgive and move on)
- Wild goose chase   (a futile pursuit not likely to yield results)

Allegories in Dreams

Allegories are essentially narrative stories that contain lots of symbols that represent people, places, or life lessons that the author wishes to highlight. Many biblical parables are allegorical in nature. Spiritual dreams are full of allegorical devices.

A spiritual dream's message is not usually transmitted in a straightforward, open manner. Rather, the dream's message is hidden in symbols, in allegorical tales, and in cryptic plays on words, dates, or phrases. So, this is why you should study Jesus' parables as practice for interpreting dreams. The same skills involved in interpreting parables (a dependence on the Holy Spirit and an ability to think metaphorically) are the same skills involved in interpreting dreams.

Spiritual dreams portray important life issues or spiritual truths but the revelation is concealed in stories involving snakes, bears, silver coins, or ships on the high seas. We must train ourselves to view animals, occupations, and common objects metaphorically and allegorically. Before we move on let's break down the parable of the two debtors as found in Luke 7:41–43. This will illustrate the principle.

> *Two people owed money to a certain lender. One owed him 500 silver coins. The other owed him 50 silver coins. Neither of them had the money to pay him back. So he let them go without paying. Which of them will love him more? Simon replied, "I suppose the one who owed the most money." "You are right," Jesus said.*

In this parable, we see a simple one-for-one correlation between common actions and objects, and what those common actions and objects signify spiritually.

the lender = God
the debtors = fallen humanity, those "indebted" to God
silver coins = our sin debt, a "price we cannot pay" on our own
forgiving the debt = God's forgiveness of our sin; an act of grace

Word Plays in Dreams

Another device I see often in dreams are what I call little word play clues. This is where part of the dream's message is revealed through a word or other phonetic device, which on the surface is not immediately recognizable. For instance, God may be speaking to you about your need to trust Him more instead of trusting in your own ability to solve problems.

Now let us suppose you have a nice colleague at work named Jennifer Preymore. It would not be out of the ordinary if you were to have a series of dream vignettes one night in which things kept going wrong. Let's say in scene one, your car breaks down. In scene two, you keep losing your temper. In scene three, you can't seem to find your way to a job interview, even though you're familiar with the streets listed on the address.

In each of the dream scenes, you keep trying to solve your dilemma and nothing works until Jennifer Preymore arrives on scene to help you. What message is God sending to you? You guessed it. Life will run much smoother if you'll release the reigns and just "pray more."

I have a family member, Lia, who has recorded her dreams for over ten years. She takes them very seriously. She once shared with me about a time she complained to the Lord about her life and her problems at her job. Soon thereafter, she was awakened in the night several times by a dream about the name "Magdalene Ursaline" or "Magdalene Usalym." The first name was very clear, but she could not quite make out the last name. When she crawled out of bed, she could not get this name out of her mind. She decided to get online and do research on the name.

She discovered the famed Magdalene Asylums of Ireland which were notorious for locking women up and taking away their freedom and identities. The Irish opened the asylums in good faith in the 18th century. They served as a refuge where former prostitutes, orphans, and others in need could work and have shelter as they were restored spiritually.

Abuses began to creep in, and eventually, many of the asylums became virtual prisons where women were used as slave labor and never allowed to return to their families. As Lia read about the tragic lives of these women, she repented to the Lord in tears and vowed to always remember this story whenever she began to have self-pity or complain about her life. In this instance, God chose to communicate a message about murmuring through a dream word play.

Names in Dreams

Another cryptic way messages can be hidden in dreams is through the use of name meanings. Sometimes we will encounter a character in one of our dreams and the person will actually introduce themselves or we'll overhear their name. Normally we don't get the benefit of having dream characters provide us with their names, so when this does happen, be sure to pay attention to that. Frequently, that piece of information is provided because it's an important clue in decoding the overall dream.

For example, let's say you have a dream in which you can't seem to get a promotion at your job no matter how hard you work. You stay late and even volunteer for the unpopular shifts, but no matter what you do your boss keeps passing over you for the next promotion. Let's say in the final scene of the dream your regional manager calls you into his office and tells you the reason you can't get promoted is because you've changed your name and the company cannot promote people with two names on file. You proclaim, "I've not changed my name!" Subsequently, your boss hands you a file showing where you did indeed change your name. Right there, in black and white, is the name change form, listing your new name as "Mary." You wake up scratching your head as to the meaning of this dream, but suppose this dream reflects reality. You really have been frustrated by your lack of advancement in your current job.

The first thing you should do after having a dream like this is to look up the meaning of the name, "Mary." When you do, you'll discover it means "bitter." A dream like this is often a revelatory dream showing you the reason God has not given you the promotion at work is because of the bitterness toward someone you've refused to forgive. Once you forgive the person and get over your "bitterness," you'll get the promotion the next time it's offered. The dream is given, along with a specific name, in order to communicate a message to you about your current spiritual state and how it's affecting God's blessing in your life.

Now, for those of you named Mary, rest assured that many names, Mary included, have both positive and negative meanings, depending on the suspected language origin of that name. The Hebrew origin of Mary means "bitter," but other Middle-Eastern origins of the name Mary reveal that it means "beloved."

Also note that God will sometimes put people you know in your dreams just to communicate a message related to what their name means. Don't just assume that every time someone appears in your dream that the dream is about them. It may just be that the dream's message is related to the meaning of that person's name.

So, anytime you hear a name clearly emphasized in a dream, you should always investigate what it means. It just may hold the key to interpreting that particular dream. I have a book in my study containing the meanings of over 60,000 names. I use this resource all the time when interpreting dreams. It's been very helpful to me over the years. Here's just a quick sample of some common names and what they mean:

Aiden	"fiery"
Asher	"blessed"
Barbara	"foreign, stranger"
Charles	"man"
Donald	"world ruler"
Isaac	"laughter"
Jessica	"God sees"
Leah	"weary"
Miguel	"who is like God?"
Sophia	"wisdom"

Types in Dreams

Finally, we must also be aware that God uses certain people in our dreams to stand for particular qualities or traits. These people are called "types" because they symbolize a "type" of issue or trait God is highlighting to us in our dream. People types may be close friends of ours, casual acquaintances, or even famous people we've never met. Therefore, when you dream of a particular person, do not always assume the dream is actually about that person. Hold on to the possibility that this may be a use of a type.

I've found that it is common for God to use types when communicating about a particular class of people he wishes you to minister to. Perhaps in some dreams the poor and oppressed are represented by an old woman you have never forgotten. Maybe you made her a meal once when you volunteered at a homeless shelter. Her image was burned into your mind from that day forward. She may appear in your dreams for many years to come because now she represents all of those who are societal outcasts, destitute, and in need of God's love.

During my high school and early college years God used the valedictorian of my high school class, Amy Clark, as a generational type. Whenever I dreamed of Amy I knew the dream was actually speaking to me about my own generation, Generation X. Somehow in my mind, I associated Amy's governance of our class (she was our class president as well) with being the "head" of our class, and thus, she represented my entire generation. She gradually faded from my dreams sometime during my later college years, but for several years when Amy would show up in my dreams I immediately knew what group of people God was speaking to me about.

I will never forget another type dream I once had. In the dream, I was driving a large garbage truck. I was jumping some hills and doing some tricks. I had it all under control and was not performing any trick that would actually endanger me. Then someone opened the door of the truck and started driving. I was now in the passenger's seat.

This gentleman began doing very risky maneuvers in the truck. At some point he backed up and floored the gas pedal and was heading toward a large mound he intended to jump. He jumped the mound alright and had us about 100 feet in the air. We went out so far that we actually went off a cliff and were now free-falling hundreds of feet, and in about six seconds, we would be crushed and killed. In my dream I turned and looked at this man and said, "Great, you know you just killed us?!" As I was falling I remember thinking about the death that would soon overtake me.

The uninvited driver in my dream was a man I was not particularly fond of. We were not close relationally, but we had some ties with one another due to a mutual organization we belonged to. This man served on the board of a well-known Christian organization. He had written many books and made regular media appearances. When I first met this man he struck me as one full of pride, going on and on about his various accomplishments. I'm sure he is a good Christian man at heart, but ever since our first experience together, I was a little turned off by him. I remember thinking, "Man, that guy has a lot of spiritual pride."

Upon waking from my dream about the garbage truck, I immediately knew that God was dealing with me about my own pride. The message of the dream was that my pride in a certain area was going to take me off of a cliff if I didn't submit that issue to God.

When the Lord wanted to communicate a message to me about pride, He knew *exactly* what person to put into the driver's seat to ensure I got the message. I did get the message, loud and clear.

Let us suppose that you very much look up to your pastor, and in many ways, he is the personification of honesty and integrity. From time to time, he may show up in your dreams as a symbol of integrity. Suppose you have a co-worker who has a problem with gossip and negativity. Everyone in the office knows when you are out of eyesight, you'll be her next victim of some character assassination. It could be that she may turn up in your dreams as a spirit of slander or a teller of tall tales. When you see her in your dreams, the dream is not about her at all; the dream is addressing a trait or issue that she personifies.

Principle #7: Dream Symbols Are Unique to Each Person

A common method in dream interpretation is to encourage people to look up a dream symbol's meaning in a standard dream dictionary. Many Christian dream interpretation resources encourage this as well. We must be very careful with this method. It has been my experience that dream symbols are highly personal and to force universal meanings on objects, colors, animals, or anything else is very limiting and can sometimes lead to shallow interpretations.

The fact is, we as individuals are so unique. We have extremely different fears, likes, prejudices, image associations, and everything else. Colors, sounds, occupations, and types of people may mean one thing to me and something completely different to another person.

Some people grew up as animal lovers and had amphibians as pets all their lives. They love turtles and lizards and grew up raising tadpoles as kids. When they see a turtle in their dreams they have extremely positive associations with them. For the child that had the end of its little pinky finger bitten off by a snapping turtle at age three, turtles are terrifying animals in their dreams and in real life, even today.

Decoding Your Spiritual Dreams

While we're on the subject of turtles indulge me for a moment while I illustrate this point. I once took a few moments to look up the meaning of "turtle." I consulted a number of popular Christian books and websites and here is what each of them had to say about what turtles symbolize in dreams.

The meaning of "Turtles" in dreams:
Turtle—peace, serenity
Turtle—an improvement in your business conditions
Turtle—slow, cautious; protection, security
Turtle—longevity, length of years
Turtle—spirit of stupor
Turtle—"sticking your neck out" (as in taking a chance)
Turtle—hiding in your shell; retreating

As we can see, these suggested meanings make perfect logical sense, and I'm willing to grant that, in some dreams, seeing a turtle could symbolize any of the above meanings (though I'm still scratching my head on the whole "spirit of stupor" one). My point is this: turtles can mean many things because so many associations can be made from them. It is best to analyze turtle imagery on a case-by-case basis for you personally where context and the overall dream's message will help you to identify their meaning in *your* dreams. If you see turtles appearing in your dreams regularly, then you will gradually learn to discern what they symbolize.

In conclusion, I am not against using dream dictionaries. I just want you to know they have their limitations and that they are not the final word on a dream symbol's meaning. *You* are the final word on a dream symbol's meaning because dream symbols are unique to the individual.

Creating Your Personal Dream Catalog

A dream catalog is simply a listing of all the objects, animals, people, or anything else that appear repeatedly in your dreams. When similar items keep appearing, they alert you to the importance of their symbolism. Once you decode them, you'll know what they mean in all of your future dreams. Well, at least until your symbols change. More on that in a minute.

I have two sets of dream symbols that represent spiritual weakness to me. The first are dirty aquariums with lethargic fish, and the second are starving parakeets. Let me explain. For many years of my life I maintained tropical aquariums. I absolutely *love* fish as pets; however, during college, I often worked two jobs to support myself. Between the fifty-plus hour workweeks and taking classes at night, some things had to take second place in my list of priorities. Properly cleaning my aquarium every two weeks was one of them.

Sometimes I would not get around to cleaning my aquarium for months. By that time my fish we're ready to pull a *Finding Nemo* on me and make a break for it. The poor little guys, I still feel guilty to this day for what I put my babies through. For those of you who don't own aquariums, let me explain. If you don't clean them often they get dirty and unsightly very quickly. The once-clear water slowly takes on a brown hue as toxins and waste build up within the water. Green algae spots, which start off microscopic and invisible, gradually grow in size and multiply like rabbits in heat. They soon take over the walls of the tank to the point that it gets difficult to see inside. As evaporation takes effect, the water level in the tank begins to drop week by week.

During seasons in my life when I would neglect my time in the word and in fellowship with God, the Lord would send me a dirty aquarium dream. I'd dream of tank conditions so horrible no fish should be able to be alive (and yet somehow they were). Upon waking, I immediately knew what the Lord was saying to me. *"Bryan, you're dying spiritually because you've disconnected from Me. Your water level is falling (Holy Spirit) and your perspective on people and life is getting very skewed (green algae on the glass; can't see). It's time for some maintenance. Come see Me."* I also used to keep parakeets as pets, and I'd dream of similar conditions about parakeets sitting in uncleaned cages while not having fresh water or food for long periods. The message was the same, God was calling me to slow down and connect with Him.

Decoding Your Spiritual Dreams

In my personal dream catalog, demons are represented by a variety of images. In my childhood, demons would appear in my dreams as big tattooed, bearded men on motorcycles. My apologies to all of you big bearded men with tattoos who happen to enjoy motorcycle riding. You see, when I was a very small child, my mother and I were harassed by a group of men from a regional motorcycle gang. It was a traumatic experience, and ever since then, that image has been burned into my head. I associate those bikers with carnal, ungodly men who live for vice and sin. When I would see burly motorcycle riders in my dreams, I knew exactly what they stood for.

In my dreams today, demons are usually represented as snakes or men with guns. When I dream of small toddlers I know I'm dreaming of new "baby" Christians. God's anointing is shown to me as bright red cars. When I dream of UFOs God is speaking to me about high, mystical spiritual experiences.

As you begin recording your spiritual dreams, be sure to include all of the recurring images you run across. As God gives you the interpretation of what these symbols mean for you, write them down. In time you'll develop a list of symbols and their meanings. It will make future interpretations much easier as you'll immediately have insight on the dream.

Now, I must also add that our personal dream symbols will change throughout our lives. Snakes may represent demons in your dreams 75 percent of the time, but God may also begin using scorpions to represent the enemy. In time, He may discontinue using snakes entirely. A well-known evangelist that you respect may represent the gospel to you for a few years, until one day you notice you have not dreamed of that evangelist for quite some time. Instead, it now appears that baskets of fish and bread represent the gospel to you. I don't know why some of the symbols change over time, but they do.

Perhaps, as we grow in our walk with the Lord, He introduces new symbols that highlight slightly different facets of the truth He's ready to show us. Perhaps, He mixes things up from time to time to keep it interesting and to keep us on our toes as we seek Him for the interpretation. Whatever the reason for this, I just want you to be aware that cataloging your dream symbols is not something you do one time. The experience of hearing the voice of the Lord in your dreams will remain a fresh experience for your entire life.

Principle #8: Ask Yourself Probing Questions About Your Dream

Meditating and asking yourself some key questions about your dream is a great exercise and will yield fruitful results. As your mind reflects on the dream you definitely want to begin looking for patterns, key themes, and an overall message. Once an overall message emerges before you, then it's time to ask yourself some important questions.

It's now the appropriate time to begin analyzing the dream on a deeper level. I have discovered the questions below to be very helpful. You certainly don't have to use them all. You may have others that are equally as helpful. Add whatever questions you feel are necessary to help you draw out the dream's meaning.

Helpful Questions When Analyzing Your Dream

1. Did this dream move me emotionally? Did I awake with a sense that this was "just a dream," or could this be God trying to tell me something?
2. What was the dominant feeling I experienced when I awoke? Joy? Excitement? Fear? Heaviness? What was I feeling during specific key scenes in the dream?
3. Was I a participant or a spectator in this dream?
4. What seemed to be the key theme, idea, or action of this dream? In essence, what is the main issue this dream is addressing?
5. Does this theme or issue relate to what is going on in my life at the present, or does this dream seem to revolve around some past issue in my life? Could this dream relate to something in my future?

6. Are there any universal, common symbols in this dream? Do any of my personal dream symbols, which I've previously decoded, appear in this dream?
7. Are there any hidden word plays on phrases, people's names, or streets that I remember from the dream? Are there any metaphors or idioms that I perceive in the dream?
8. Who were the people in this dream? If I know them, what does that person represent to me? What does their name mean? Are they positive or negative in my life? Is this dream actually about one of the people who appeared, or could they be a type?
9. What do I feel this dream is instructing me to do? Is there an attitude I need to change or an idea I need to open up to? Is there a person I'm supposed to pray for or talk to?

Principle #9: For Difficult Dreams, a Gifted Interpreter Is Helpful

As I've mentioned before, most of the time God will give us the interpretation to our spiritual dreams. We must simply be patient and be willing to wrestle with them a bit. It's part of the privilege we have of coming before our Father and asking Him for the revelation we need to better serve Him and carry out His will.

However, many of us have been at that place where we know we've received a dream from Him, but we are truly stumped in trying to discern its meaning. At some point it is appropriate to seek a fellow believer in the body of Christ for whom God has granted the specific spiritual gift of dream interpretation. These brothers and sisters will be a huge blessing to God's people as they use their gift in decoding the really cryptic dreams we get from time to time.

I want to encourage you, however, to not be too quick to ask for help. Don't rob yourself of the extreme pleasure of having God reveal a dream's meaning to you. I feel people are too quick to want an answer rather than digging out the truth for themselves. The searching, the praying, the "a-ha!" moment that finally comes are personal victories to be enjoyed.

I will also say that there are times in which you most certainly want to run a dream past a gifted interpreter. This is especially important for calling dreams in which you ask God to confirm a significant revelation He has shown you—one which might require major lifestyle changes.

Closing Thoughts

To help you remember the essential principles of decoding a dream, consider using the "FRAME" acronym. By listening to the Holy Spirit and using these five steps, you'll remember what is necessary to discern, or "frame," the meaning of a dream.

F – **Feelings**. What dominant emotion did the dreamer experience? Joy, fear, sadness?

R – **Reduce** the dream to its simplest form. What is the main plot? What are 2 or 3 sub plots?

A – **Ask** follow up questions to the dreamer, if needed.

M – **Metaphors**. Any metaphors, idioms, colors, name meanings, etc. showing up?

E – **Encoded** symbols. Any universal symbols present? Decode the universal and other symbols.

In closing, let's briefly review the nine principles. As you become aware of these truths moving forward, I promise you will begin to understand your dreams at a much deeper level than you've experienced before.

- **Principle #1: Dream Interpretations Come from God—** We can grow adept at recognizing common symbols and some themes are obvious, but many dreams have hidden, deeper meanings that are only revealed by the Holy Spirit.

- **Principle #2: Pray for the Interpretation of Your Dream** — Immediately after waking and recording the dream, our next order of business is to ask God for insight into the dream's meaning.

- **Principle #3: Examine Your Feelings and Emotions During the Dream** — Each dream will leave us with specific emotional reactions, either positive, negative, or neutral. These emotions are half of the key to interpreting the dream.

- **Principle #4: Identify Your Place in the Dream** — One of the first things we need to do in analyzing our dream is to determine if the dream is about us or someone else. Our place in the dream as either a participant or a spectator will easily confirm this.

- **Principle #5: Reduce the Dream to Its Simplest Form** — No matter how many scenes a dream may contain, or how complex it appears on the surface, there is a single message beneath it all crying to be heard.

- **Principle #6: Dreams Are Cryptic and Symbolic** — A dream's message is hidden beneath layers of symbols. These symbols can sometimes take the form of extended metaphors, idioms, word plays, or types.

- **Principle #7: Dream Symbols Are Unique to Each Person** — Resist the urge to depend solely on standard dream dictionaries. Dream symbols and their meanings are unique to each person. Over time, we can catalog our symbols and create our own dictionaries that are completely accurate because they are revealed to us personally by God.

- **Principle #8: Ask Yourself Probing Questions about Your Dream** — We can help draw out a dream's meaning by asking ourselves some very specific questions.

- **Principle #9: For Difficult Dreams, a Gifted Interpreter Is Helpful**—For really difficult dreams be encouraged that God has blessed some in the body of Christ with the gift of dream interpretation. They will prove a blessing to you in searching out or confirming a dream's meaning.

Chapter 7

Common Symbols in Spiritual Dreams

ALTHOUGH I STAND FIRMLY behind the statement that dream symbols are highly personal, there are at least a few symbols that seem to have a universal meaning. In the many dreams I've interpreted over the years, I consistently see about two dozen symbols with the same meaning to people, regardless of their diverse backgrounds and experiences. I want to caution you that these individual symbols could still have a different interpretation from what I'm listing below, but it would be the exception, not the norm.

For you analytical readers who want a more precise statement as to how reliable these universal symbols are, I'd feel comfortable saying that in 80 percent of the cases these symbols reflect what I will share below. Let us now explore the meaning behind a select list of very popular images which appear in dreams all over the world.

house—a person, their life, their spiritual state; the present condition of one's life

This is probably the single-most popular symbol I see in others' dreams. When a person dreams they are entering a house and interacting with it, they are actually seeing a symbolic portrait of themselves. Perhaps this is because we spend so much time in our

Common Symbols In Spiritual Dreams

homes. We eat there, sleep there, play there, and interact with our closest friends and family there. Our homes are, in a very real sense, an extension of ourselves. It seems quite natural that God chooses to use the home as a symbol of our very lives.

This idea even has scriptural support. In Matthew 7:24, Jesus uses the symbol of a house to represent a person. He states that those who build their "house" on the rock will not be tossed to and fro when the winds beat down upon it. The house He speaks of is, of course, a word picture representing the person's life. In Matthew 12:43–45, Jesus is teaching people how demonic spirits enter and exit their victims. He then shares a hypothetical conversation one demon has with another. The demon makes it clear he desires to enter the person again but instead of calling his host a "person," he says instead, "I will return to the *house* I left."

When decoding house dreams, pay attention to the feelings you have while in the house. Is the house warm and inviting or does a heaviness fill its rooms? Is it in ill repair or well-kept and beautifully decorated? Pay attention to the condition of the house and any other objects or items that stand out to you.

A common theme I find in house dreams is a person discovering a new room within their house. It's as if behind the water heater they suddenly stumble upon a door, and they are excited to explore a room they never knew existed before. If associated with a positive feeling, this is usually a very good dream that speaks of God opening up a new area of ministry or a new area of your life which had previously never been developed.

I've also interpreted dreams in which a hidden room was discovered, but the feelings associated with it brought fear or shame. This could mean God is exposing a dark side of yourself or a secret sin you've not been dealing with, hidden from everyone else. The dream in this version is meant to shake you from your apathy so you will act on what you've previously not been willing to deal with.

I once interpreted a dream in which a woman kept finding money hidden in the walls of her home. She would come home and accidentally bump into the wall where a hole would then appear. To her amazement, she would find bundles of cash lying in the framework. She kept having this dream over and over in various forms. When

I spoke with her about it, I had some good news and some bad news for her.

I shared with her that the bad news was that I did not believe the money represented actual money that would soon come her way. The good news was that the money represented treasure or value yet undiscovered within her. She needed to pray and ask God what she was neglecting in her life which God placed great value on. She had become oblivious to it. She later shared with me that God had indeed showed her exactly what the money in the walls represented. She was very excited once she discovered what this issue was that she had long neglected. She made some significant changes in her life, including breaking off a relationship that was not right for her, and was blessed and happy after obeying the revelation the Lord gave her through the dream.

Another woman once shared with me that she dreamed of arriving home one evening and as she was walking through her front door she noticed a man coming down her stairs. He was handsome and had golden hair. He was dressed in all white and appeared to be a painter who was there to do repairs and give the house a fresh coat of paint. He was kind and peaceful and she felt no fear as she watched Him walk through the house inspecting it room by room. This was a wonderful confirmation dream depicting that Jesus (the man in white) was doing a work in her life (symbolized by his "work" in the house).

In the popular house dream, it is also not uncommon for the main action of the dream to be focused on the furnishings. I recall one dream in which the person was invited to view two homes with two very different sets of furnishings. One home had beautiful, fancy furnishings while the other home was very modestly decorated. Strangely, both houses were completely underground and just the tip of them protruded from the yard above, although once inside they looked like any other home and had all the conveniences one could ask for. An unknown man then asked the person to choose which house they would live in.

The interpretation I received was that the Lord was asking this person to choose what kind of Christian they wanted to be. Would they be one whose house, or whose "life," would be filled with heavenly treasures (represented by beautiful furnishings) or would

Common Symbols In Spiritual Dreams

they instead settle for filling their life with the common things of the world?

The fact that both houses appeared underground revealed that this dream was actually speaking specifically about foundational issues in this person's life. The foundational elements and furnishings they decided to put within their home (their life) would ultimately determine the way their life would be lived out in the long run. Upon hearing this dream, the verse that the Holy Spirit quickened to me was 2 Timothy 2:20–21, *"In a large house there are articles not only of gold and silver, but also of wood and clay; some are for noble purposes and some for ignoble. If a man cleanses himself from the latter, he will be an instrument for noble purposes, made holy, useful to the master and prepared to do any good work."*

Once we are wise to the fact that the home represents a person, it is not too difficult to then decode the secondary elements that appear in the dream. For instance, if the focus of the dream is on the floor or the condition of the floor, this often speaks of foundational issues related to that person's life. Windows can often speak of that person's perspective or how they view things. A cloudy window that barely allows one to see the outside is a negative symbol pointing to a skewed perspective or isolation. A roof speaks of covering and protection. Dreaming of attics speaks of the past or things that have been neglected or forgotten. Furnishings oftentimes reveal the "things" we fill our life with.

If in the dream you are in someone else's house, then that house will represent that person. If you dream of your childhood home, then that dream is pointing out issues related to your past or related to that time in your life. Anything that stands out to you should be prayerfully considered. What catches your eye in the dream, and the corresponding feelings associated with your experience, will guide you toward the key elements in common house dreams.

car—how well (or not) a person is progressing in life; the current condition of one's life; one's personal ministry

Cars, trucks, and other small capacity vehicles represent the current capacity of the person to move successfully through life;

thus, they are barometers of our relational, spiritual, or vocational health as we travel our "journey of life." They can sometimes represent the person, but usually vehicles have the specific nuance of representing how one is living while traveling down their personal "road of life."

When you dream of driving in a fast-moving car with the wind at your back, and you have masterful control of the vehicle, then that is a good sign. If, on the other hand, your car can't get out of first gear and tops out at a snail's pace of 10 mph then you're being shown a life that is currently "stuck" and not operating at peak efficiency.

Dreams in which our car crashes are alerting us that we are not being successful in regards to a certain aspect of our life's journey. The dream is symbolically communicating that our present course is a "wreck," and we "can't move forward" any longer until something is addressed in our life. What could that something be? Well, that's where prayer is vital. If the answer is not immediately obvious, then we must ask the Holy Spirit to show us where we've traversed off path.

I remember a dream I once interpreted in which a man was driving down the interstate. As he was looking through his windshield at the road before him, all of the sudden the road faded away and he found himself viewing the Grand Canyon, although he was still driving down the highway. This was God communicating with him that his horizons were going to be expanded. Instead of the mundane old road he was used to traveling as he went about his life, God wanted to show him grand vistas and massive expanses of creation wrought by the hand of God. This was an encouraging dream and was told through the common symbol of one's car, which again, usually represents the forward progress of the dreamer.

I have discovered many dreams in which the person is always the passenger in the car, never the driver. This is usually a negative symbol because it speaks of being too passive. Someone else is directing your agenda and you are simply "going along for the ride." When this dream occurs careful attention ought to be placed on who is doing the driving and the feelings you experience while in the passenger's seat.

Are you feeling anxious and resentful that you are not doing the driving? This dream will often appear over and over from time to time until you take control of your life and make the necessary changes. Once you correct your course and take responsibility for your own life and actions, the passenger dreams will fade away.

Sometimes, however, we delude ourselves into thinking we can actually control our life and everything in it. Sometimes God will give us a dream in which a mysterious man (Jesus) will arrive on the scene, take control of the car, and will drive it for us, taking us to places unknown or to destinations we've desired but have been unable to get to. In these dreams, we don't feel anxious or angry; we feel relieved and thankful. This would be a good dream, and the context would let us know we arrived at the intended meaning God had for us. Heaven's message to us: "Step aside; it's time to let *Me* do the driving."

large capacity vehicle (bus, train, airplane)—same meaning as the "car" symbol above except now representing associations of people such as one's family, a church, one's co-workers or company, etc.; one's personal ministry

Large capacity vehicles show us the current path or direction of groups of people. Dreams utilizing these symbols will reveal information that affects more than just a single individual. Large capacity vehicles and cars can still sometimes represent our personal ministry. To dream of a church member who suddenly pulls up in the middle of a service and loads half of the congregation onto a bus he is driving would indicate that this person is an influencer, and people are following him. If later in the dream that same bus has a horrible wreck, and bodies are tossed all over the road, then we must carefully and prayerfully ask God for the proper interpretation of this dream. Variations of this dream are not uncommon.

Two possible interpretations would logically fit here. On one hand, this dream could be positive. Suppose the leadership of the church had recently been praying about planting a new church across town. Let's say they have not yet made this plan public to the larger congregation. Then, one Sunday, a church member relays this bus dream to the pastor. It deeply worries her, and she feels the dream relates to their church. The church leadership should pray over this dream and ask God for its meaning, especially if the person has an established track record of receiving accurate prophetic insight.

It could be a warning dream where God is revealing the plans of the enemy who wishes to destroy this new congregation (the tossed bodies flung from the wrecked bus) before it can take ground for the gospel. In this case, through prayer and intercession, the plans of the enemy will fail and that congregation will not only avoid a wreck, but thrive!

On the other hand, let's say the church has no plans of planting a new church, yet this same bus dream is shared with the leadership. In this case, the dream could also be a warning dream. However, in this dream, the Lord is revealing ahead of time that a certain person in the church is planning to usurp the pastor's authority, leave, and take many families with him. The end result is that this person (the bus driver) is taking this group (passengers on the bus) and God has not blessed this move because it stems from rebellion. The end result is that many of the families riding the bus will be hurt, disillusioned, and ultimately spiritually harmed.

Sometimes particular vehicles may represent the current state of a group or organization. For instance, one might dream the company they work for picks up its employees for work each morning in a sleek corporate jet. It's all smiles and everyone is happy. Later, that same company announces a new policy that everyone will continue to be picked up for work each morning, but now they'll arrive via the company mule train. These mules look like they've not been fed in weeks.

A dream such as this would probably portend a decline in that company's fortunes, or at least a decline in how it treats its employees. Context would have to determine the meaning, but simply recognizing the universal vehicle symbols would take you far down the road in interpreting the dream. The passengers in the vehicle will alert you to who this dream is about. If it's folks from your church, the dream is speaking about your church. If the passengers are all people you work with, the dream is speaking about your company or organization.

Very large capacity vehicles, such as trains, often represent Christian denominations, or other very large church movements. Vehicles that fly, such as commercial airliners, do sometimes represent corporations or businesses, but they just as often represent ministries and church movements. This is because these particular vehicles move through the air, and the air and wind are both symbols of the Holy Spirit.

Lastly, I must add that sometimes airplanes and other flying vehicles have the added emphasis of achieving something great. They can sometimes refer solely to an individual and not a group, so be especially attentive to the other details of the dream here. When in an airplane, the message is sometimes that the individual is "flying high in the Spirit" and "soaring above" all obstacles as they walk in God's will for their life.

flying—the current progress toward some goal, the current level of mastery or victory attained in relation to some issue or season of life; moving high in the Spirit

When we dream of flying we must pay special attention to how well we're doing it. This is an exhilarating dream that many have had. When we dream of storm clouds or violent thunderstorms below us, yet we are unaffected by them because we are powerfully flying high above them, then this is a very positive dream. Our Lord is reassuring us that while turmoil may be going on all around us, we are promised a victory because, through His power, we will simply sail above the storms and arrive safely to our ultimate destination.

A common deviation from the popular flying dream is the one where we are barely flying, often just a few feet or a few inches off the ground. Our efforts to move forward are labor intensive, and we are not at all graceful. This speaks of the current reality of our situation in which we are not experiencing victory in a specific area where God wants us to "soar."

Decoding Your Spiritual Dreams

Flying dreams can also signal those who will move powerfully in prophetic ministry. Moving through the air (Spirit) in these dreams can indicate that God wishes to use the dreamer in ministries that showcase God's power and presence.

Some people have even dreamed of flying in outer space. In these dreams they move powerfully and majestically through the atmosphere, and they find they can even breathe in outer space. This is a very positive dream. Of course, context must rule, but usually this signifies that if they remain faithful on their present course, God eventually wills that they move into very high levels in the Spirit and in His Kingdom.

This is the kind of dream where you get very excited that you got it, and then you get a sobering realization of the steep price you will be required to pay in order to see it actually come to pass. Dreams such as this ought to drive us to prayer and deep reflection. They require a significant lifestyle change to match the requirements of the call. A heavenly invitation such as this is special indeed.

nakedness—(if associated with embarrassment or other negative feelings) vulnerability, powerlessness, shame, being exposed; (if associated with positive feelings) intimacy, transparency, exclusivity

When we appear naked in our dreams, it is either a very positive symbol or a very negative one. Our feelings and the scenario we find ourselves in during our dream will quickly help us know which interpretation to apply to this common symbol.

In the Bible, nakedness has two very different associations, depending on the context. Nakedness is repeatedly used in a negative way to speak of those in sin or those outside of God's covenant (see Isaiah 47:1–3 or Ezekiel 16:35–38). In other passages it portrays innocence, spiritual ecstasy, or those in covenant relationships blessed by God (see Genesis 2:25, 1 Samuel 19:23–24).

Most of us would feel embarrassed and at a loss of power if we were suddenly laid bare in front of our friends and co-workers. This symbol carries over quite literally to represent much of the same thing when it happens in our dreams. A common naked dream involves someone giving a presentation or hanging out with a group of friends only to look down and suddenly discover themselves in nothing but their birthday suit! Upon this discovery, they are shocked and humiliated. This reveals that in some aspect of their life they feel "exposed" and vulnerable or, they feel this way toward the group that appears in their dream.

On the other hand, not all dreams of nakedness cause feelings of anxiety or shame. Sometimes dreams of appearing naked are followed by feelings of peace, joy, or wonderment. Within this context the dream is quite positive. Once a young man came to me with a perplexing dream in which he and a close friend were walking down a long hallway with many closed doors off to the right and left sides. The young man and his friend opened a door and saw Jesus standing majestically before them in a white robe. The dreamer looked at Jesus with awe.

Jesus calmly walked toward them, removed His white robe, and stood naked before them. At that moment, the young man fell to the ground in reverence. His friend just stood there but took no posture of subservience before the Lord. Then he woke up. As you can imagine, the dream un-eased him a bit. On the surface, it seemed sacrilegious. Why in the world would he have such a horrible "dirty" dream of Jesus taking His clothes off in front of him when he entered the room?

The Lord immediately gave me the interpretation. His dream was not bad, but rather very encouraging. I felt the Lord was telling him that he had to make some decisions. His so-called "Christian" friends were compromising the way they lived their lives. At their current commitment level to Christ they would never experience the kind of intimacy and power God wanted for them.

The response and posture of the two young men symbolically represented their individual level of fear and reverence for the Lord. One observed the presence of God but was not moved. The other fell quickly to the floor, recognizing he was on holy ground. I told this teenage boy, if he followed through with the commitments he had purposed in his heart, that he would walk in a level of intimacy with God that would be enviable. When Jesus disrobed before him, it was a symbolic way of portraying the exclusivity and intimacy He desired in their relationship.

Now that we've addressed these two deeper meanings of the nakedness theme found in dreams, we need to address another issue. Yes, sometimes seeing nakedness in dreams does not represent powerlessness or intimacy, sometimes it just represents plain old nakedness as found in common sexual dreams. If we are struggling with an attraction toward someone it is not that out of the ordinary to have a sexual dream about that person. This is usually not a spiritual dream or a demonic dream, but simply a natural dream arising out of our own subconscious mind. In cases such as this, what should we do upon waking?

Well, if the person in the dream is not your spouse, or if you are unmarried and find yourself having sexual dreams about someone, my advice is say a prayer to guard your heart, take a cold shower, forget it, and go on with your day—don't beat yourself up about it. Most of us will have these kinds of dreams from time to time over the course of our lives, and sometimes there is no discernable reason why they occur. If, on the other hand, you find yourself having inappropriate dreams about the same person over and over, it could be an indication of a soul-tie forming. In that case, we must go before the Lord and ask Him to break it and protect us from a possible trap by the enemy.

the human body—revelatory insight into particular aspects of our life, ministry, or spiritual state

When particular parts of our bodies stand out to us in a dream, then we are being given a message. The message can vary greatly depending on which part of the body is highlighted. Let's explore the most common body parts that show up in dreams, and the meanings they typically convey. We'll start from the top of the body and work our way down.

hair—spiritual covering; wisdom; glory, anointing; a barometer of spiritual health

eyes—the condition of one's soul; one's perspective, how one "sees" things; prophetic ability, a "seer"

ears—the ability to hear God's voice; sensitivity to the Spirit

nose—discernment, the ability to evaluate and analyze a matter

mouth/voice—one's confession; one's level of influence, one's voice (as in one's authority to speak into a matter and be heard by others); a barometer depicting one's ability to speak/minister to others about spiritual things

breasts (female)—spiritual influence or teaching passed from one person to another; an invitation for increased relational intimacy (platonic or spiritual); sexual intimacy

arm—strength, power; the ability "to do work" *Note: The left hand/arm points to what one was born or destined to do. The right hand/arm points to what one has the strength or faith to do. Using the opposite hand/arm as one's normal proclivity (i.e. a right handed person using their left hand in a dream, can also indicate operating outside of one's comfort zone (a positive thing) or operating in a situation that is "not the right fit" for them)*

hand—the "work of one's hand", the work and activities we engage in; our ministry

genitals (male or female)—spiritual reproduction, to multiple one's ministry or influence; sexual intimacy that is blessed; to offer oneself to another outside of covenant, i.e. sexual lust

thigh—the core of one's "strength", one's character or dominant trait; covenant

leg—one's "walk" (lifestyle, pursuit of their endeavors), an indicator as to the level of strength and/or power to conduct one's "walk"; one's ability to move and go after that which they seek or desire to do, the ability to gain forward momentum toward a goal or calling

feet—also one's "walk"; peace; the endurance one has (or not) to continue in their "spiritual walk"; one's direction or course in life

eating a meal with someone—to be associated with someone, to have a relationship with someone; to be equated with them in rank, purpose, or lifestyle; to minister to someone; to provide someone with spiritual sustenance

To dream of eating with someone is often a symbolic portrait highlighting that a relationship, association, or other connection has been established with that person, or that such an association will be forthcoming (Mark 14:22–25). Eating with someone denotes relationship and a desire for closer affiliations with that person.

If the dream shows you eating with people of questionable morals or people you know to be involved in rebellious lifestyles, then the dream is likely a warning dream that you have root issues in your life that are "of the same spirit" as those you are dining with. This revelation is meant to jar you so that you will repent and not fall into the same trap they fell into. There are numerous instances in scripture where the Lord prophetically illustrates His displeasure with a person or persons by commanding His servants to not eat with them (1 Kings 13:7–10, 1 Corinthians 5:9–11).

We must, however, use discernment when interpreting dreams because sometimes seeing yourself eating with such people is not a rebuke at all. It's actually a confirmation dream that the Lord will soon open a door for you to minister to that person or that group of people. It is very common to have a spiritual dream where you are interacting with others in a cafeteria or perhaps enjoying a meal in someone's home. Context must lead you, but often those dreams are highlighting issues of relationship or issues of people who need to be spiritually "fed" or strengthened. In such dreams the Lord is calling you to be the person who will feed them.

To dream of breaking bread with someone and you suddenly notice spiders or other undesirable insects coming out of their food would of course indicate spiritual influence or teachings that have been corrupted in some way. Those in the dream do not realize that what they ingest as spiritual food is actually spiritual poison, and will end up harming them if they persist in eating from that source.

To dream of a famous effective, Spirit-filled pastor or minister offering you a seat at their meal table is a very positive dream. This dream would be a prophetic dream indicating that the Lord sees you in the same class or sphere as that powerful man or woman of God. If you continue to be faithful to God's will for your life, the dream is indicating one day you'll have a "seat at their table," that is, you will move in similar realms as they do.

teeth falling out—existing in an unhealthy environment (spiritually, emotionally, or physically); loss of wisdom; loss of power

This is a very common dream symbol that you'll run into pretty quickly if you start hearing the dreams of others for any amount of time. There are several variations of this dream. Sometimes the person's teeth have been slowly rotting, and while barely hanging on, are about to fall out at any moment. It's a very disturbing dream to anyone that's had it. While even negative symbols can sometimes be positive, I've personally only interpreted a handful of dreams where this symbol was positive. It's one of those images that almost always portends something bad, something unhealthy, or something which the dreamer needs to address before their life can be brought back into proper balance.

I liken teeth falling out dreams to people undergoing chemotherapy. When someone undergoes chemotherapy their hair falls out. The two go hand-in-hand. When God, or your subconscious mind, tries to get your attention about an unhealthy environment you're currently in that needs to change, then you're a prime candidate for a teeth-falling-out dream. When you get this dream, the only real question is, what area of my life does this pertain to? The location and people around you will be your clues as to what this dream is pointing you toward. Who is around you? Friends? Family? Co-workers?

Now, we must also be careful to not read too much into a teeth falling out dream because there are two other meanings that share this same symbol—a loss of power or a loss of wisdom. Teeth have cultural and biological associations with age and wisdom. As we progress from toddlers to children we lose our teeth and get new ones. Later, in our teens or early twenties, we yet again gain wisdom teeth, which signify another stage of life development. Teeth metaphorically represent wisdom and understanding in such phrases as "she needs to chew on that for a while," meaning she needs to think it over. So, it's quite common for teeth in dreams to signify age, wisdom, or our ability to understand things. So sometimes, when a person dreams of their teeth falling out, it simply means they lack wisdom, discernment, or understanding about the particular scenario portrayed in the dream.

Teeth also perform another extremely important function: they allow us to chew our food, which then gives our bodies the nutrients necessary to stay alive. They are, therefore, related to the ability to have power to live, work, and function normally. So sometimes teeth falling out represent a loss of power. It could be, for example, a loss of power in a one-sided relationship or a loss of power in our daily work at our present place of employment.

snake—demon, Satan, evil; danger, a bad omen; deception

When snakes appear in our dreams, it is usually a very negative symbol representing the dark forces of Satan and his kingdom. The Bible uses this symbol repeatedly, and in almost every case, the context is sin and darkness. We see in the third chapter of Genesis when Satan arrives to tempt Eve, he chooses the form of a snake. In Numbers chapter 21, when the people complain against God and Moses, what animal is sent as divine judgment against their sin? Deadly serpents. They are almost always omens of judgment, sin, or evil.

When decoding your spiritual dreams involving snakes, it is important to see the role they play in the dream and to examine the relative power they hold over us or the person we are dreaming of. If, in the dream, one is attacked by snakes but they pick them up, break them into pieces, and toss them aside, this is a positive dream indicating a current or future attack of the enemy will be unsuccessful.

However, if one dreams of a giant snake leisurely eating them, and the person is unable to break free, then the meaning is clear. Satan is slowly "sifting" them, and they are currently powerless to stop it. It's not uncommon for some to dream of playing with snakes. Perhaps a woman dreams of small snakes she keeps in her purse as pets. Whenever she grabs an item from her purse, her pet snakes bite her and draw blood, but she seems to think it's cute, not harmful. This dream is sending a message that the person is "playing with sin" or entertaining sin and not realizing that a specific activity or lifestyle choice is actually harming her.

alligator—evil, hidden danger, demon; generational sin; long-standing entrenched darkness relative to a particular person, place, or sphere

Alligators are almost always negative symbols in dreams. If you've ever seen one up close, you'll have no problem understanding why they command immediate fear and respect. They are massive animals that can grow to a length of 20 feet and can weigh up to 2,000 pounds. They can move in both water and land, day or night, and their powerful jaws can easily rip a person to shreds in a matter of minutes. Alligators kill people by rolling them over and over again until their victims run out of breath. Thus, in essence they kill their victims by taking their breath (spirit) away. They are contaminators and destroyers of one's spirit.

In dreams, they have the same dark connotation of sin and evil as do snakes but with this caveat—alligators have a deeper, secondary meaning of hidden danger, and sometimes generational sin or sin entrenched for long periods of time. Perhaps God uses the symbol of an alligator for generational or longstanding sin due to the survivability of alligators themselves. They are, literally, a species that has survived unchanged for thousands of years.

I have no wish to get into philosophical arguments regarding the age of the earth and if the days in Genesis chapter 1 are literally 24 hour days or if they represent an epoch of time, but secular scientists say alligators are over 150 million years old, having survived the catastrophe that wiped out the dinosaurs over 65 million years ago. Whether they are thousands or millions of years old, these animals know how to survive. They are very bad omens when they appear in your dreams.

A common dream with alligators would involve a person walking along a path when they suddenly notice several alligators lurking toward them. This often speaks of a person finally having to confront some issue of generational sin that is now intersecting their life and threatening to pull them into the same issues previous family members have succumbed to. Seeing alligators approaching could also represent an unseen attack of the enemy that is soon coming their way—an attack that has been in the making or "brewing" for a long while. Sometimes, the attack can be avoided through prayer, but sometimes it cannot, because it's being allowed by God because of sin or for other consequential reasons.

In those cases, the dream is meant as a warning to pray and prepare for a difficult season that will manifest. Rather than get discouraged, take heart. God is showing the person the dream, so they will not be caught unaware. Instead, through prayer, He will carry them to victory on the other side. How could we possibly grow spiritually, how could we ever build up "stories of faith" in which God delivered us if we were never allowed to go through anything difficult?

In alligator dreams, carefully examine the people appearing in the dream and the location, as this develops the context for whom and where this warning is to be applied.

horse—strength, power; an escalation in spiritual warfare, battle reinforcements

Horses usually represent one of two things when they appear in dreams. Context will help you quickly determine which interpretative path to explore. Horses primarily represent strength, vitality, and power. Before the industrial age, the raw power needed to move an object was often described in terms of "horse power." We still use this phrase sometimes today, as in "a 5,000 horse power engine." For thousands of years these powerful animals carried their human riders across great distances. They pulled chariots in battle, carriages in peacetime, and other heavy objects men were unable to move. Strength and power are synonymous with these creatures still today.

Their secondary meaning in dreams is related to spiritual conflict. The Bible consistently portrays horses as game changers in battle and associates them with the ability of one power to project its influence and authority upon another through brute force (Ezek. 26:11, Micah 5:10, Rev. 9:9) Thus, when horses show up in spiritual warfare dreams, they often denote that a battle is heating up or escalating. The horses in the dream could be from the enemy or could be heavenly reinforcements sent from God. If it's the latter, it often indicates the Lord is "sending in the cavalry" to secure victory in this present attack.

A sister in the Lord once shared with me that she was having recurring dreams about a beautiful white horse and an offer to ride it. In one dream, a person presented her with several riding ribbons. She tried to refuse them by protesting, "I didn't win these; I don't deserve them." The person insisted she take them anyway. In another dream, a massive white horse appeared with a silver mane. She then heard a voice command her, "Get on him."

She struggled to get on the horse but finally did. It took off with such power that it amazed her. All her troubles seemed to fall away as she rode this powerful, majestic animal through a field. As she was riding, she noticed the path in front of her was obscured by the horse's massive neck and thick mane. She had to trust that the animal would carry her safely.

After she told me the dreams, I asked her, "Have you been asking God recently for strength and guidance?" She affirmed that she most certainly had. She had been praying explicitly for those two things because of some very troubling issues in her family. She had been crying out for God to help her.

I then told her, "God has answered you. The white horse is Jesus. The riding ribbons presented to you symbolize the grace of God. You're right. You didn't earn them, and you never could, but they are being offered to you because grace is God's *unmerited* favor on our behalf. The voice you heard is the voice of the Holy Spirit telling you to give the reins to Jesus. The horse represents power (God's power) in the situation you are facing. It also represents God's desire to 'carry you' through this season (heavenly guidance).

The fact that you can't see the path ahead symbolizes your journey of faith. Faith means trusting God, even when you can't see everything before you." This was a gracious dream given to a child of God who cried out to the Lord for assistance. In this instance, the Lord used a common color appearing in scripture, white, to clue us in that this horse was not of man and not of the earth. This was a heavenly steed.

water—the blessing of God, the presence of the Holy Spirit; humanity, familial relationships

If associated with a positive feeling, water often represents God's presence. I once interpreted a dream of a woman who found herself carried across the bottom of the ocean by a gentle current. As she passed below, she could breathe, feel the sand passing under her fingers, and enjoy the serenity of the experience. She arrived safely on the shore under the sun where angels greeted her. The dream was a picture of the Holy Spirit gently carrying her to new horizons. She was enveloped by His presence and was literally being "carried along by the Spirit."

Water can sometimes point to the current level of purity in the Spirit associated with churches, individual Christians, or church or ministry movements within the body of Christ. If you dream of a church with a stream running through it, but you notice it is full of dirty water with dead insects, gravel, and other impurities, then that is obviously a negative symbol.

The life of the Spirit, and/or the revelation coming through that house is not what it should be. The source of that church's or ministry's motives is questionable at best, or downright corrupt at worse. Insight such as this is given so we might pray for that church or ministry.

Scripture repeatedly uses the symbol of water to represent the Holy Spirit. In Exodus 17:5–6, we see a picture of the living waters of the Spirit flowing forth from the rock when Moses taps it with his staff. A powerful picture of growing deeper and deeper in the Spirit can be seen in Ezekiel's vision of the temple river in Ezekiel 47:1–12. In John 4:14, Jesus uses water as a symbol of the Holy Spirit when he tells the Samaritan woman, *"Whoever drinks the water I give him will never thirst. Indeed, the water I give him will become in him a spring of water welling up to eternal life."*

Before we move on we must also consider that sometimes water can represent humanity as a whole. Think of the phrase, "a sea of humanity." Finally, water will often show up in dreams highlighting issues of close familial relationships, such as a child in contrast to their parents, or a person in relation to their siblings. Jesus informed Nicodemus in John 3:3–5 that unless a man is "born of water and of the Spirit," he cannot enter the Kingdom of God. The water here could be a reference to the birthing process when a woman "breaks her water." So, we see that, even in scripture, there is a link between water and kindred relationships.

taking a test/back in school—a time of preparation and impartation, a reflection of your current progress and development in your ministry calling; a current or upcoming life "test," a spiritual or natural promotion; the need to learn a skill for a new season of life or for a particular aspect of your life

This is a fairly common dream. I'm sorry to give you twenty-seven options for what this dream can mean, but the reason I do this is because . . . well, there are about twenty-seven things a "back to school" dream could be trying to tell you.

The key to interpreting back to school dreams is to examine the emotions you had when you received this dream. Are you nervous? Do you feel unprepared? Do you know the answers to the test, or do the questions read like ancient hieroglyphics and you have absolutely no clue how to answer them? If that's the case, then we all know this is a negative dream, possibly a warning dream or a portrait dream confirming some unresolved issue rising to the surface.

Negative test dreams simply alert us to the fact that we feel "unprepared" and "unable to measure up." They can signify an area of our life where we're not able to advance because there is some skill, knowledge, or understanding we must possess that we currently have not acquired.

I get this dream from time to time, and I hate it. It absolutely stresses me out and depresses me. In my dream, it's the end of the semester, and I suddenly realize I've done my school work in some classes; however, there is usually one or two classes in which I've completed almost none of the assignments. I kept putting off work in those particular courses, and now it's time to pay the piper.

I haven't completed the readings, haven't written the required papers, nothing. The last day of class is coming up in a week or so, and I suddenly realize there is no way I'll get all the assignments done; it's just not physically possible given the time left before grades are due. These dreams relate to aspects of my calling I've not yet fulfilled but should have by now. I've neglected the disciplines related to those aspects of my calling, and when the grades are due, I know I'll soon be earning a big, red "F." For me, these school dreams are portrait dreams, especially painful portrait dreams that vex me greatly.

If one has to return to school in the dream but walks up and down numerous hallways unable to find their classroom, this reflects the person's stress over uncertainty about how they will acquire the skill or understanding they need. They can't even find the source (the teacher), so how will they ever improve their lot in life?

In other variations of the dream, you might find yourself in a large classroom taking a test. What stands out to you is the large clock hanging on the wall. You watch the second hand slowly making its way around the clock face. What could this mean? It means you have a limited season or "time" in which to act if you want to pass this test. If you do what you know you have to do, then when the time comes, you'll have finished the test and will be promoted to the next grade. Or, to extend this to your actual life, if you do what the Lord has asked you to do, in the time He's given you, then at the end, you'll be promoted spiritually and advance to the next grade (the next level of your spiritual development).

police officer—authority, civil government; law, order; protection; spiritual authority, angels

Common Symbols In Spiritual Dreams

Seeing a police officer in a dream is a fairly common occurrence. When police officers appear in dreams they are usually highlighting issues related to civil authority or governmental issues. They can also appear simply to represent the concept of authority in general. It's still not uncommon to say, "call the authorities" as a substitute for "call the police." Thus, the Lord will often use these public servants to represent this general concept.

In addition to functioning as agents of the state, it's not uncommon for police officers to represent spiritual authority as well. Since uniformed officers are granted a measure of authority over ordinary citizens, and since their primary function is to serve and protect us, they can also represent spiritual or angelic forces. They will often arrive in our dreams, deliver a message to us, or order us to do something, and then return from where they came. Sometimes the presence of a police officer in a dream will simply be to highlight the concept of protection. Therefore, police officers can represent a variety of themes and concepts, but luckily, their presence in dreams follows very closely with their actual functions in society. So, after considering the overall theme of the dream, it is not too difficult to determine what concept they are likely representing.

money — talents, resources; provision; access, favor; to have influence with a person or organization

When money appears in dreams the message very often centers around one of two themes: blessings and resources or favor and access with others. A dream's context will quickly help us to determine which of these issues the Lord is highlighting.

When we dream of finding money this is in an indication that good things are on the way. Provision, either physical or spiritual, will soon arrive on our behalf. Money can represent actual money that will soon materialize or it can just as often represent other resources that will help us excel in our personal, ministry, or business life. Money can sometimes represent spiritual gifts that will be discovered or imparted to us. Money is, in its most basic sense, a "medium of exchange" and thus in dreams it can represent the gifts and abilities that you will "exchange" in your interactions with others as you go about your life.

When we use money we are in essence having "dealings" and "interactions" with others. These dealings are with churches, restaurants, or with the dozens of companies we give our money to when purchasing their products. When you dream of money passing between you and a company, ministry, or other person this is often a prophetic dream indicating that you will soon have favorable "dealings" or "interactions" with that organization or person.

The Lord will sometimes give me a dream in which a ministry leader or business person gives me a large sum of money to deposit in a bank on their behalf. Sometimes the ministry leader hands me bank bags full of gold coins or sometimes it might be bundles of company issued checks that need cashing. The metaphorical picture here is that this ministry or person is essentially trusting me with what is precious to them (the "fruit of their labors" or their "store of wealth"). When I receive this dream I know that the Lord is tipping me off that in the future I'll have access and dealings with this person or ministry. The Lord is giving me this dream so that I will pray for them and be ready to serve them. When the time comes that our paths cross I will know to give this encounter my time and attention because I know it's a divine appointment, not a random chance encounter.

elevators, escalators, and stairs – (ascending) a spiritual or natural promotion; favor, advancement; a positive new experience is on the horizon; a time of transition is at hand; (descending) spiritual or natural progress that is being stalled or hindered; lack of favor, access, or advancement; a negative reversal of fortune is upon you; a time of transition is at hand

These symbols fall under the "simple coded" category. They mean what you would expect. To see yourself advancing to a higher place is a very positive symbol indicating promotion and positive new experiences coming your way. If this occurs on an elevator pay special attention to which floor number you get off at, for often the specific floor is germane to the dream's interpretation.

To dream of being on an escalator that breaks down and is then unable to take you to your destination is a negative symbol indicating something is "broke" and until it's addressed you'll not experience any significant progress. I once interpreted a series of dreams from a person who kept dreaming of being at work and every time she attempted to use the elevator it would break or some other issue would arise that would prevent her from getting to higher floors.

This young woman had tried numerous times to get a promotion at work, but at every attempt she was overlooked for the promotion, even though she was a very smart, capable individual. I had to share with her, "you are not going to get promoted at this organization. The dream is revealing that you don't have favor with this group of leadership. As long as they are in power, your elevator will not advance to the higher floors."

storms (tornados, hurricanes, lightning storms) — spiritual warfare, the forces of God, the forces of Satan; the intersection of physical and spiritual forces; an approaching dark or difficult time, a bad omen

When storms show up in your dreams, it is often a symbolic depiction of the intersection of natural forces (people, governments) with spiritual forces (angels, demons). Thus, storms or any phenomena that occur in the sky such as clouds, lightning, or stars, highlight spiritual forces at work. Jesus makes the metaphorical linkage between storms and spiritual forces when He commented in Luke 10:18, *"I saw Satan fall like lightning from heaven."*

Storms can also serve as bad omens pointing to a soon-approaching time of judgment or a difficult time ahead. Western culture collectively associates storms and natural disasters with divine providence or judgment. This is demonstrated in common insurance policies that contain "acts of God" provisions which release the insurer from all liability due to damages caused by floods, tornadoes, or earthquakes.

Context will determine if the storms represent heavenly or demonic forces. For instance, I have interpreted many dreams where an approaching tornado is white. In almost all of those dreams it signified that the coming "shaking," or storm, was from the Lord, not Satan. The spiritual event portrayed by storms could be positive, as in a coming move of God that will usher in great change, or it could be negative, like a Satanic attack upon a particular group, community, or nation.

Many Christians, including a close friend of mine, had dreams of airplanes crashing into things or tornados striking large cities in the weeks before the terrible September 11th, 2001 attacks on our nation. In these instances, the tornado dreams represented what they typically do: a spiritual attack and a soon to arrive "storm."

light—revelation, understanding, the ability to know or perceive; God, spiritual understanding; natural understanding

It's fairly easy to understand why this particular dream symbol carries its unique meaning of enlightenment. It's one of those symbols common in both scripture and our own culture. Numerous verses in the Bible equate light with God (John 8:12, James 1:17), and our own culture, for over a century, has equated light with understanding. What's the very symbol of a breakthrough in understanding in many Western countries? You guessed it—a light bulb.

When interpreting dreams involving the concept of light, always first check to see if the theme of the dream involves understanding, revelation, or an emphasis on perceiving spiritual things. Many times, you will find that God encodes dreams with some sort of light when He's highlighting issues of perception or revelation. Sometimes, the dreams will involve actual fluorescent lights, while other times the lights will be natural involving the sun or stars. Sometimes the dream will contrast two different sources of light, such as sunlight versus a flashlight to highlight a contrast between God-given revelation versus man-centered revelation.

gold—holiness, godliness, heaven; wealth, treasure, value; idolatry

The color gold is used often in scripture to denote holiness and heaven. Job 23:10 speaks of enduring God's testing that we may later "come forth as gold." In Revelation 4:4, the twenty-four elders that surround the throne room of God will all wear crowns of gold.

Of course, gold also denotes wealth and treasure. It has served as a medium of exchange for over 5,000 years. Therefore, when we see gold in our dreams, it is usually a very positive symbol. This symbol can take on its spiritual meaning of godliness or its natural meaning representing wealth or value.

I remember interpreting a dream many years ago in which a woman saw a gold face. This man's face was literally dripping gold. The man pointed to two people who were standing off to the side of her. I interpreted the dream and told her that the man with the golden face was Jesus (His face represented the glory of heaven for he was literally a "golden man," i.e. a man of great value). The two people in the dream represented two types of people that this woman would be ministering to in a greater way in the future. Years later, God indeed gave this woman a very effective ministry with these specific groups of people, just as the dream had revealed.

If someone were to dream of walking along a street only to discover a golden path behind some weeds that led to a golden rock, then that dream is obviously very positive. It just may mean that the person will soon come into a great store of resources or wealth. Dreams of gold are a good indication that the dreamer has good fortune, either spiritually or materially, coming their way in some measure.

silver—redemption, grace, sanctification; wealth, treasure, value; greed

Silver and gold are twin metals and twin colors often associated with one another in biblical narratives. Silver, like gold, has a natural meaning of wealth and value. Like gold, it has a spiritual meaning relating to God and heaven. When you dream of gold, you've arrived in heaven. When you dream of silver, God's doing a purifying work to get you there.

In all seriousness, silver has a connotation in scripture of redemption and sanctification. In ancient times one would heat up silver where the impurities inherent in the metal would rise to the surface. The master silversmith would then scoop those impurities away leaving a pure, easily malleable and beautiful metal. This metal was prized by others and served as a store of value. Scripture speaks of purifying and redeeming us like silver in such passages as Psalm 66:10, Malachi 3:1–3, and 2 Timothy 2:20–21.

When silver shows up in dreams, look to see if part of the message is speaking of God's grace or a redemptive, purifying work that may be coming. If one dreams of a person walking through a silver door, then that very color may be showing us God intends to use this upcoming experience to refine some aspect of that person's character.

Or, perhaps someone dreams they look down only to notice their hands have turned entirely silver. Depending on the context, the person may soon be coming into some material treasure, or they may be getting ready to be involved in some type of restoration or grace-based ministry. In this dream, the hands may signify "work" while the color of the hands signify the type of work which will be done, namely "redemptive work."

black—judgment, sin, darkness; a bad omen; power, authority

The color black is often a negative symbol when it appears in our dreams. There are a few scriptural uses of this color as well. In Genesis 1:2, a black darkness covered the formless and empty earth before God began His creative works. The prophet Jeremiah incorporates this color when speaking of the judgments against Israel (Jeremiah 14:2), and Revelation 6:5 also uses the color black to denote judgment.

If a man wearing all black were to approach you in a dream, it often signifies a coming judgment or shady character that should not be trusted. Of course, we must also be aware that black is sometimes a positive color as well, especially in the world of finance and business.

When a company is profitable again or coming out of its budget woes, it is said to finally be "operating in the black." Oil, one of the most precious commodities on the planet, is often referred to as "black gold." Dreams of a black liquid, such as oil, can be positive, indicating a coming financial breakthrough.

The color black also symbolizes formality, power, and authority, so sometimes this color shows up to highlight those characteristics as well. A man dressed in black beckoning you to follow him into a previously locked room, could signify someone of influence and authority. This person could have the authority to grant you access to something previously off limits. This is a perfect time to reiterate that context must ultimately determine any symbol's meaning.

white—purity, holiness, godliness; a good omen; a legalistic, religious spirit

The color white has biblical associations of purity and holiness and therefore is often a positive symbol when it appears in our dreams. Isaiah 1:18 speaks of God taking our scarlet sins and making them "white as snow." Revelation 4:4 speaks of the twenty-four elders in heaven being "dressed in white," and Revelation chapter 20 tells us that Jesus will one day judge the entire earth while seated on a white throne.

Even though white is almost always a positive symbol, I feel I must again emphasize that we cannot get too comfortable assigning standardized meanings to colors or any other dream symbol. Revelation 6:8 speaks of a pale horse (off-white) that arrives at the end times and represents the sword, famine, and a worldwide plague! Canned formulas will fail us. Ultimately, we must depend on the Holy Spirit to give us the meaning of a dream's symbol.

The Symbolic Meaning of Colors

In our discussion of common dream symbols, I included four colors I see repeatedly in dreams: gold, silver, black, and white. Those four colors almost always represent the meanings I described above, but what about other common colors that appear in dreams? I've discovered many other colors do have some common associations with people, but I don't think they are quite as standardized in their meanings as the other four I mentioned previously.

With that said, I want to share with you how the Lord uses other common colors and what they *typically* represent in dreams. These other colors, however, can have a wider range of meaning based on an individual's association with those colors or their unique cultural context. In essence, I would feel comfortable saying the meanings I will share below are accurate about 65 percent of the time for those who grew up in Western culture and nations. Also note that most colors have both positive and negative associations attached to them. Without further ado, here are the meanings of some of the most common colors appearing in dreams:

clear, translucent – relating to spiritual things or spiritual beings; God, angels, demons

white – purity, holiness, godliness; good fortune; clinical; a religious, legalistic spirit

black – judgment, sin, darkness, fear; bad fortune; power, authority

gold – holiness, godliness, heaven; wealth, treasure, value; idolatry

silver – redemption, grace, sanctification; wealth, treasure, value; greed

red – anointing; redemption; love; anger, conflict; sexual lust; caution, cease, stop

yellow – happiness; remembrance; a gift; the soul, the mind; cowardice

orange – harvest, fruitful; sociable, community; preparation, evaluation; (Amber) God's glory or presence

gray – mature, wise; undecided, neutral; morally questionable or compromised; weakness; unhealthy

purple – royalty, high social rank; rarity, exclusivity; anointing; creativity; corruption; worldly leadership; the occult

green – vitality, growth, healthy; undeveloped; proceed, go; envy, jealousy; nature

blue – spiritual, heaven, of God, the spirit; prophetic; depression, sadness; calmness, tranquility

brown – earthy, natural; humanistic, relating to mankind; clergy, ministry; decaying; the body

The Symbolic Meaning of Numbers

Before we close our discussion on common symbols, we need to address the numbers that also frequently appear in dreams. As we study the Bible we notice that there are noticeable numeric patterns that emerge throughout the text. This is a subject, however, that has been debated in the church for over two thousand years.

Some Christians are adamant that the Bible does not ascribe any special meanings to numbers and to look for them is a foolish exercise. The reason for this is because some New Age religions focus heavily on numerology, and thus some Christian leaders don't want any of these associations creeping into the church.

I have never been a fan of the theological equivalent of "throwing the baby out with the bath water." I mean, where do we draw the line with such simple thinking? Sex in the bounds of marriage is a beautiful God-ordained gift, but it can be abused. Do we teach our people to abstain from all sex because non-Christians sometimes abuse it? The gift of tongues can be abused. Do we forbid all speaking in tongues on the basis that if we allowed it, it could *possibly* be abused? We could go on ad infinitum, but I think you get the point.

Many teachers in the church believe strongly that all numbers have symbolic spiritual meanings. For those of you who are called to have a ministry of dream interpretation, this is a topic you will have to form an opinion on eventually. So, let's explore it.

I find biblical numerology to be an interesting subject. If you pressed me to take a position on this issue, I'd tell you I believe there is some truth that numbers can have a spiritual significance, just not to the extent that is taught in some circles today. From my study of God's word, I do not see a detailed theology taught or implied by the Old Testament prophets or the apostles in the New Testament regarding special qualities or meanings behind numbers.

There are no commands or exhortations calling us to study numbers, search out their meanings, or to focus on them. However, there is an exception, and it's a pretty significant one. I am referring to the church's warning about the future arrival of the anti-Christ.

>We are specifically told what his "number" will be when he arrives:
>
>*This calls for wisdom. If anyone has insight, let him calculate the number of the beast, for it is man's number. His number is 666.* Revelation 13:18

So, while I do not believe every number under the sun has some deep, layered meaning, I do believe the Bible insinuates that some numbers have both a natural and a spiritual meaning. Revelation 13:18 could not be clearer; it even assigns the number "6" to correspond with mankind.

So I'm of the opinion that there are a handful of numbers used repeatedly throughout scripture that do indeed carry a spiritual meaning. When we see these numbers in dreams, we can be confident that we will understand the deeper meaning they carry with them.

The Number 6

This is identified in numerous passages as being the number associated with mankind. It is not always a negative number as some would suppose. Positively, it can simply refer to mankind in general, or negatively, to the aspects of sin and the flesh, which are associated with man's fall from grace.

- Man and woman were created on the sixth day (Genesis 1:27–31)
- Noah was 600 years old (a multiple of 6) when the judgment flood came on mankind (Genesis 7:6)

- 6 cities of refuge were established because of man's vengeance (Numbers 35:6)
- The sixth commandment prohibits man from killing man (Exodus 20:13)
- The mark of the beast, the number of man, is 666. (Revelation 13:18)

The Number 7

There is one number in the Bible that even the critics have to admit has special significance to God, and that is the number 7. The number 7 is a special number, symbolizing spiritual perfection, completion, or fullness. God has layered both the Old and New Testaments with this number so often, I will only touch on a few examples. Note how significant this number has been throughout God's redemptive history.
- God created the world in six days, rested on the seventh, and blessed that day above all others, calling it the "Sabbath." (Genesis 2:2–3; Exodus 20:8–11)
- Noah was to take on the ark 7 pairs of every clean animal (Genesis 7:2)
- Israel's disobedience would be punished "seven times over" (Leviticus 26:18)
- Jericho was delivered to the Israelites as they marched 7 times around the wall on the seventh day (Joshua 6:4)
- Solomon built the temple in 7 years (1 Kings 6:38)
- The apostles commission 7 deacons in the early church (Acts 6:3–4)
- 7 churches are examined by the apostle John (Revelation 2:1–3:22)
- John's revelation includes 7 angels, 7 spirits, and 7 seals (Revelation 1:20; 4:5; 5:1)

The Number 12

Twelve is another number that appears frequently in both the Old and New Testaments. This number carries the meaning of spiritual rule or governance.
- There were 12 tribes of Israel (Genesis 49:1–28)
- The priest's ephod contained 12 stones (Exodus 39:14)
- When Israel left Egypt they encamped at Elim where there were 12 springs (Numbers 33:9)
- The temple altar of Ezekiel's vision is 12 cubits long and 12 cubits wide (Ezekiel 43:16)
- Jesus selected 12 apostles (Matthew 10:2–4)
- The apostles will sit on 12 thrones in heaven (Matthew 19:28)
- At His arrest Jesus says He could call on 12 legions of angels (Matthew 26:53)
- Heaven will have 12 gates and 12 foundations (Revelation 21:12–14)

The Number 40

This number also appears quite frequently throughout the Bible, so we know there is a spiritual significance to it as well. The number 40 is associated with a spiritual test or trial, which if passed, will cause one to advance in their relationship with God.
- Noah believed God about the flood and was spared. It rained for 40 days and 40 nights (Genesis 7:12)
- Moses was faithful to God and stayed on the mountain with Him for 40 days and 40 nights (Exodus 34:28)
- The children of Israel have their faith tested by spying out the land for 40 days (Numbers 13:25)
- The children of Israel fail the test and wander in the desert for 40 years (Numbers 14:33)
- Goliath, mocking Israel, tested their faith by appearing for 40 days (1 Samuel 17:16)
- Nineveh would be destroyed in 40 days if they did not repent (Jonah 3:4)

- Jesus was tempted by Satan for 40 days in the desert (Luke 4:1–2)

So we see that there are definitely a handful of numbers used repeatedly in scripture, and they very much have a symbolic meaning attached to them. This is irrefutable. The problem lies with extending this pattern to other numbers. Numbers are mentioned throughout the Bible, and they occur in literally hundreds and hundreds of verses, but it is very difficult to make the argument that the Bible associates these other numbers with concrete spiritual meanings. There is just too much diversity in these texts to make hard and fast pronouncements.

Personally, I do believe other numbers show some significant patterns, and I use these insights in my personal interpretations. Often, I get solid confirmation from those I'm ministering to regarding my insight into the numbers that appeared in their dream.

So in this issue of assigning spiritual meanings to other numbers, I must leave to you. Take this before the Lord in prayer as you consider what I've shared. There have been many proposals offered regarding what other numbers might signify. I'll share with you some meanings that have general acceptance in the modern church. For the record, I believe these meanings are accurate and I use them in my own ministry of interpreting dreams. Note: some of the numbers have both positive and negative associations, hence the apparent contradictions.

1 – God; singular; unity
2 – confirmation; division, separation; a choice that must be made
3 – the Trinity, God; firmly established; divine design
4 – the earth; creation aspects related to the earth and universe; totality, universality
5 – protection, deliverance; blessing through spiritual obedience and faith; grace; God's dealings with mankind; works; bondage, legalism
6 – mankind; of human origin, human effort; carnality, flesh, sin; weakness
7 – holy; spiritual perfection; of divine origin, purpose, or design

8 – covenant, promise; renewal; a new cycle or era; eternity
9 – fruitfulness, fullness of the Spirit; judgment
10 – order; completeness; human government; to measure; a representation of the whole
11 – incomplete; not fully ripened or finished; near the end; transition; judgment
12 – divine government; godly rule and order; spiritual authority
13 – rebellion, revolution, apostasy; man-centered order and authority

The Key to Decoding All Other Dream Symbols

Now that we have looked at the most common dream symbols, the question before us is, "What about everything else?" We know what houses, cars, snakes, and alligators represent. What about office buildings, libraries, trees, and dolphins? What does it mean when I dream of rocks, jewels, and gas stations?

I am seriously considering a second book on dream interpretation where I expound on hundreds of other symbols, because quite frankly, there is so much we could explore together. This work will only scratch the surface, but until that time, let me simply give you the interpretive key for everything else. Here's the secret:

> *In any given culture, a dream symbol's meaning is most likely tied to the closet metaphorical associations that can be applied to that symbol.*

What is air? It's invisible. We can't see it, but without it, we cannot live. It fills us. When it's blown over us, it refreshes us. It gives us life. God breathed it into our Spirit in our very beginning (Genesis 1:7). What is one of the most common symbols for the Holy Spirit in the Bible? Air, wind.

What is a mobile phone? A device for communicating. It's a device that takes communication and causes it to travel invisibly "in the heavens" from point A to point B. What do phones often represent in spiritual dreams? "Heavenly" communication or "hearing" from God.

On and on and on I could go but if you will listen to the dreams of God's people for any length of time you will continually see what I've discovered in over twenty years of interpreting dreams. God uses common objects, colors, occupations, and natural phenomena to speak to us in our dreams. Because revelation is precious, and because it's not meant for just anyone, He veils His messages by speaking to us in riddles, mysteries, and, yes, in metaphors.

Therefore, if you want to understand your dreams at a very high level, you really only have to do three things:

1. **Study the Word of God** where He reveals many of His favorite metaphorical devices to us already. Rocks = Christ. Air, wind, water = Holy Spirit. Birds = harbingers. Serpents = Satan and his dark kingdom.
2. **Learn to think metaphorically** so that you'll have a head start in understanding symbols which are not mentioned at all, or are not emphasized, in the Bible. This would include symbols like cell phones, skyscrapers, and dolphins.
3. **Maintain a close walk with Jesus** so that you have the discernment to perceive how the Lord is using a symbol in any given dream.

Now of course this leads us back to the fact that the reason I don't put as much faith in dream dictionaries is because so many different associations can be made from the same symbol. The Lord will use a particular symbol in your dreams because He knows how you feel about that symbol. He might not use that same symbol to mean that in my dreams because I don't have the same associations for that symbol.

However, we must also realize that millions of us do have similar associations with really common symbols. Therefore, there is a high probability that the most common symbols will mean the same thing to all of us, or at least to most of us. So things like: cell phones, office buildings, highways, airline pilots, and gold coins will typically still serve as near universal symbols for the messages the Lord relays to us in our dreams.

You are likely more skilled in metaphorical thinking than you realize. It's just a muscle that has to be worked. To prove it let me test you. I'm going to give you five symbols that I have not covered in this book and you are going to prove to yourself that you already know what they mean. As you consider the scene or symbol, think about what it really represents. Think about the logical associations.

The answers are on the first page of the next chapter.

1. When the Lord warns us about a sin that is "entrapping" us, what animal might He use to encode that information?
   A) a wolf
   B) a spider
   C) a bear
   D) an earthworm

2. When the Lord wants to speak to you about the nation of Russia, what animal might He use to communicate that message?
   A) a lion
   B) a bear
   C) a hawk
   D) a seal

3. If you dream of the Lord presenting you with a powerful, golden sword, and in the dream He says, "Learn to use this, and you will be victorious." The Lord is most likely telling you to focus on:
   A) spending more time in the Word of God.
   B) starting a ministry to unwed mothers.
   C) changing your membership to a new church.
   D) becoming a powerful deliverance minister who will overcome demonic forces.

4. When you dream of being led to a library and are told you must check out a specific book, what is the Lord most likely highlighting to you?

Common Symbols In Spiritual Dreams

A) That you must learn to go wherever He leads, no questions asked.
B) That knowledge of His Word is more important than worldly knowledge.
C) That there is a false teaching being spread in a book and you will find it and expose it.
D) That a season of learning is upon you and God will soon direct you to a specific resource.

5. You dream that you are wearing a white physician's coat and on your right arm is a patch with a cross on it. You hear sirens in the background and know that in a few minutes badly wounded patients will start arriving. What does this dream likely mean?
A) God is calling you to attend medical school and begin training as a physician.
B) God is calling you to not be ashamed that you are a Christian and to proudly "display" your cross (your faith) at work.
C) God is calling you to be sensitive to those who are hurting.
D) God is calling you to minister to spiritually wounded people that He will soon bring to you.

Chapter 8

Inviting God into the World of Your Dreams

Answers for the Chapter 7 quiz: 1. B, 2. B, 3. A, 4. D, 5. D

EVERYTHING WE HAVE LEARNED thus far will help us better understand and interpret our spiritual dreams, but is there a way we can actually increase the occurrence of spiritual dreams in our lives? I believe so. Once we start receiving spiritual dreams or begin to see them increase in our lives, I believe there are some things we can do to properly respond to that revelation. Below are some truths that will help you achieve both of these aims.

Ask God to Speak to You in Dreams

James 4:2 tells us, *"You do not have because you do not ask."* The passage goes on to tell us that we often don't get what we pray for because we ask with the wrong motives. God looks on our hearts. When we ask our Father to speak to us because we want to hear His voice and obey, then that, my friend, is a request God will honor. Our Lord wants to speak to His children. Receiving a spiritual dream is not only an exciting thing, it's a very practical thing. We all want more clarity in knowing His will, and dreams help us achieve that. If the Lord knows we will obey the dreams He gives us, then He will grant us more of them.

Again, I truly believe that most of us have had spiritual dreams in the past, but we've simply not recognized them. I'm guessing that is a mistake you will not make again. So, begin tonight asking in faith for God to speak to you in your dreams. Then, get ready. I believe He will do so. You might even want to say a prayer like this:

Father, I want to know Your will for my life. I want to be a better servant. Show me things, teach me things; reveal to me what I need to know in order to do that. Lord, I want to be open to any way that You wish to speak to me, but I also want to hear You in my dreams. Please speak to me this way. And when You do, help me understand and obey. Speak to Your servant in the watches of the night. For I ask this in the name of our Lord Jesus Christ and for His glory. Amen.

Maximize Your Ability to Get Restful Sleep

Remember, we learned in chapter 5 the average person will achieve four or five REM cycles a night. The latter REM cycles last longer than the earlier ones. So, if you are cheating yourself and only getting five or six hours of sleep a night, you are depriving yourself of prime "dream time" each night.

I know there are seasons in all of our lives where the recommended eight hours of sleep just isn't practical, but try to get as much sleep as you can because it will help you dream. Some studies have shown that the body does a majority of recharging and recovery between the hours of 11:00 P.M. and 1:00 A.M. There is a reason most people went to bed shortly after sundown prior to electricity, and it is still a good idea today.

So many folks want to unwind after a hard day's work by watching television late into the night or surfing online. We all need our outlets, but taking a look at our evening habits, I believe most of us can get to bed a little earlier each night. It will not only help us cultivate more time for dreaming, but we'll be more rested the next day as well. Here are a few additional ideas for fostering better sleeping habits and attaining a deeper sleep.
- Establish, as much as possible, a regular bedtime. Going to bed and waking up at the same time every day helps

the body get into a rhythm that encourages deeper, more restful sleep.
- Enjoy the relaxing effects of a hot bath, shower, or sauna before bed. Some sleep experts cite the value of raising the body's temperature in encouraging deep sleep.
- Listen to soothing white noise or relaxing music to help you wind down for the evening.
- Exercise regularly. Studies show that exercisers generally fall asleep easier and experience deeper sleep. However, avoid exercising too close to your bedtime.
- Avoid drinking fluids within an hour or so of going to bed. This helps reduce bathroom visits during the night which interrupt sleep cycles.

Find what works for you. If you need assistance, contact a physician who specializes in sleep techniques. Remember, the key is finding ways to maximize sleep time, thereby providing ample opportunity to receive as much uninterrupted dream time as possible.

Record Your Dreams

Most dreams are wiped from your memory within one to five minutes upon waking. It's crucial to record your dreams immediately as soon as you wake up. Don't take a shower first. Don't you dare get that cup of coffee yet! Attend to the dream *first*. Trust me, if you wait around, the details will fade in minutes. Remember, when it's a spiritual dream, it is divine revelation. Treat it as such and show God you respect what He has just given you.

Do you know how many times I've woken up with a very vivid spiritual dream only to get very discouraged when I roll over and realize it's 3:30 in the morning? I'm tempted to say, "Why, Lord, why?" I get out of bed and write it down because I know that if I wait until morning, I will have lost many of the finer points of the dream or even large chunks of it. There have been times when my flesh got the best of me and I did roll back over and went back to sleep. "I'll remember this one. No way I can forget it." When morning came I could not recall all the details. That is information lost forever.

Bill Gaither is an incredibly talented and prolific Christian songwriter. Gaither has won multiple Grammy and Dove Awards. His classic compositions include, "Because He Lives," "He Touched Me," "There's Something About That Name," and a string of others. A friend of mine interviewed him once and shared something with me that I will never forget. He told me that the Lord would give Gaither some of his songs while he slept. Gaither told him, "The sad thing is that there are so many other songs probably better than 'He Touched Me' and 'The King Is Coming' that I simply didn't get up and write down. By the morning, I had forgotten them completely."

Let this be a teachable moment for us all. Some people like to write out their dreams longhand. Some folks prefer to use their computer. Others have found it more convenient to invest in an inexpensive digital recorder which they keep by their nightstand. They get up, dictate the message, and commit it to paper later when they have some free time. However you choose to record the dream, just do it.

Spend Time Reflecting on Your Dreams

When God gives you a spiritual dream, it makes sense to spend time digesting and assimilating the details and message. You will undoubtedly discover that each new dream draws you into a deeper relationship with Him. Discover what He wants you to understand. This is why journaling is so vital, but I encourage you to go even deeper after journaling. As you ponder what He has given you, be sure to ask Him for clarity and direction. Take time with God. Cherish those times. Then, don't be surprised if He pours out even more of a spiritual harvest upon you and your life.

As you read over past journal entries, you may begin to notice certain symbols, words, and emotions that occur again and again. As you pay attention to these patterns, however slight, you may begin to notice important details you might have otherwise missed.

This is especially significant as you dream in the future and begin realizing that God has been giving a unified message, dream upon dream. Sometimes, you don't notice these details until you detect the recurring patterns in your dreams.

Also, be aware that these patterns may change as you become more aware of what God is telling you through spiritual dreams. I can tell you from experience that God weaves beautiful dream tapestries, but sometimes you don't understand how magnificent they are until you see a more cohesive pattern develop over a period of weeks, months, and even years.

Act on Your Dreams

Finally, it's not enough to receive a spiritual dream. What we want to do is show the Lord that we're also acting on them. I believe if we'll obey the voice of the Lord in our dreams, He will be pleased to grant us additional dreams in the future. James 1:22 exhorts us, *"Do not merely listen to the word, and so deceive yourselves. Do what it says."* This verse has application for any form of revelation God would give us. It doesn't matter if the message comes from His Word, from a teaching, a dream, or any other avenue of His choosing. When God speaks to us, we need to listen and obey. If you will do this, you can expect to receive more revelation. Much, much more.

Chapter 9

Protocol for Dream Interpreters

AS THOSE ON THE front lines of this ministry, we want to ensure we understand the biblical role of dreams and what the scriptures have to say about them. I believe God is raising up modern-day Daniels and Josephs to help both believers and non-believers understand these heavenly messages.

However, as with any spiritual gift, there is potential for this gift to be abused. So, we must establish some basic standards for those who are called to a ministry of dream interpretation. We, as dream interpreters, must demand accountability from each other and the church must know we take our gift seriously and exercise it responsibly before the Lord. Let us now explore some foundational principles that will help us better steward this unique gift.

How Do I Know if I Have the Gift of Dream Interpretation?

This one is easy. If you truly have the gift it will be confirmed over time. People will share their strange and cryptic dreams with you and you'll tell them what those dreams mean. They'll either excitedly confirm your interpretations are correct, or they'll look at you, politely thank you, but you'll know in your heart of hearts that what you told them didn't really resonate. I know that look very well. It's the look I still get today when I've blown an interpretation.

The first indication of a true dream interpretation gift is that you'll be a fairly consistent dreamer. You'll typically get dreams every week or at least several dreams every month. I don't know any dream interpreters that are not regular dreamers themselves. Not only will you dream regularly, you'll be able to interpret most of your dreams fairly easily and consistently. Some interpreters get the interpretations instantly and some have to mull over them for a bit.

The next progress marker is when you start hearing the dreams of others. If you can pretty much do with others, what you do with your own dreams, then you have the gift. The only question left to answer is what level of anointing are you currently operating at. There are some dream interpreters who can decode extremely complex dream sequences, and they are accurate 95 percent of the time. Those are the men and women who are very highly skilled in the gift. Most of us don't operate at that level. I certainly do not. I would venture to guess that historically I'm able to interpret about 70 percent of the dreams I receive. For the rest, I simply hear the dream, stroke my chin, and say, "where's John Paul Jackson, when you need him?"

In the early stages of development, the best thing one can do is to hear as many dreams as possible. The more dreams you hear and the more you can practice, the sharper your gift will become. So, listen to the dreams of family members, neighbors, co-workers, and people in your church small group. This is the only way to grow in your gift.

If you consistently offer accurate dream interpretations, then you can be confident that this is a gift the Lord has given you. You will now just need to be open to using it to serve and bless the church. Again, this gift, like any other spiritual gift, will be confirmed over time.

Record Your Interpretations

It's important to keep a record of the interpretation for any significant dream. This is easy to do for dreams received in writing or electronically. Interpretations taking place in the midst of a church service, conference, or small group are just as easy to document with the aid of simple digital recording devices.

The recording process is important for two reasons, not least of which is to protect the reputation of the interpreter. Can you imagine the fallout that might occur if someone were to foolishly quit their job and move their family across the country, only to begin some failed ministry enterprise? The person might be tempted to proclaim, "That's what that dream interpreter said God wanted. They told me God required me to take a step of faith right now!" What if the dream interpreter had said no such thing?

What if she simply said something along the lines of "I feel the Lord is opening up a new door of ministry for you on the East Coast, and I think it's coming soon. Pray about this and see what the Lord might speak to you concerning the details." That's a lot different from, "Thus saith the Lord, you're to move to New Jersey immediately!" If the interpretation were recorded, there would be no question that it was the dreamer who acted presumptuously, not an interpreter giving quick and easy prophetic advice that cost her nothing to dispense.

Not only do recorded interpretations provide a layer of accountability for the interpreter, they also protect the dreamer from reading more—or less—into the interpretation. Let's face it, with time, all of our memories fade, details get fuzzy, and years later, we might think we remember certain details of the interpretation that were never actually there. A simple recording or written interpretation easily clears this all up.

I realize there are times when providing a recorded interpretation just isn't possible or convenient. I certainly don't want to be legalistic and demand that, unless a pen and pad can be rounded up, we shouldn't offer an interpretation. I realize interpretations sometimes occur in the midst of a conversation on an airplane or at a park when God sends us a divine contact.

I also realize that most dreams deal with very common issues that don't involve major life changes, so there would be no need for such a formal capturing of those kinds of interpretations. I am certainly not suggesting that I provide a written record of every single interpretation I give, but for significant dreams dealing with career changes, moves, or major ministry advice, I make a real effort to ensure my interpretations are recorded word for word. I do this both for my own protection and for the protection of the dreamer. I want that person to be able to share my words with others when praying over the matter. A written or recorded interpretation ensures a factual account of what was shared.

Have the Dreamer Weigh the Interpretation

Another good practice in dream interpretation is to always counsel the dreamer to weigh any interpretation we give. This is especially true for dreams that require or propose significant actions or lifestyle changes. Significant dreams like these should be shared with one's pastor or elders or someone in spiritual authority in their local church. It goes without saying that the person should share any significant dream with their spouse.

When the dream's contents are shared, along with the offered interpretation, the individual, their spouse, and their spiritual covering can pray together seeking God's will on the matter. This is another check against a hasty interpretation. Remember the wisdom of Proverbs 24:6b which exhorts us, *"in a multitude of counselors there is safety* (KJV)." If all parties feel confident the dream and its interpretation are from the Lord, then that individual can have peace about moving forward on the revelation received.

However, before that person brings our interpretation to their spouse or elders, we ought to first find out if our comments bear witness with their spirit. This is the first thing I want to know after I give an interpretation. I'll ask the person, "Did this feel right to you? Did I hit the mark, or do you feel I missed the meaning of this dream?"

I believe the dreamer is the final judge on whether the interpretation is accurate or not. If it is, it will resonate in their spirit. It will move them or affect them in some way as God confirms the dream's meaning. When the dreamer tells me he or she didn't bear witness with my interpretation, then I encourage them to pray more on the dream and find someone else who might have different insight. More times than not, I get confirmation from the dreamer that my insights are accurate, but there are times when this isn't so. Those times remind me that I'm a vessel of clay fitted for service by a gracious God, not a spiritual superstar who never makes a mistake.

Revelation, Interpretation, Application

Another important factor every dream interpreter must be aware of is that when we hear a dream there are three separate issues we must take into account. Every dream will contain a revelation, an interpretation, and an application.

The dream itself is the revelation. To understand revelation we first must learn to listen very carefully when another person is speaking. Once we've heard the revelation (the dream) and asked any follow up questions we need to clarify our understanding, then we move to phase two—the interpretation. This is where we listen to the Holy Spirit and we offer what we believe to be the meaning or interpretation of that particular dream. Once this is accomplished we have one other factor to deal with—the application.

For most dreams the application is self-evident. If a dream speaks of a person slowly decaying spiritually because they've failed to forgive someone who has hurt them, then the application is obvious. They need to begin forgiving that person so they will thrive spiritually again. Sometimes a dream's application is not so straightforward. In Genesis 40:16–19 Joseph correctly interprets the symbols of birds eating from a man's head as a symbol that someone would soon die. Who would die? It was Pharaoh's food, so would the dream point to Pharaoh dying in three days? Or does the dream point to the baker of the bread? In this dream Joseph was accurate not only in his interpretation (the dream means someone will soon die) but was accurate also in the application (that someone is the baker).

Oftentimes a dream interpreter will offer an accurate *interpretation* but will offer up an inaccurate *application*. So, just because you feel confident that the Lord has shown you the meaning of the dream, don't automatically assume you know exactly how that revelation is supposed to be applied to that person's life. Oftentimes the dreamer will be more skilled than the interpreter in knowing how to apply the revelation. So interpreters should not presume to know how that dream should be applied. If the Lord gives that insight then great, but don't assume you have that insight just because you correctly interpreted the dream.

Speak When God Speaks, Be Silent When God is Silent

There will be times when the Lord uses you greatly in your gift, and it seems as though no dream is too difficult to decode. You may be amazed at the insight God gives you as you are able to call forth the Lord's plans and purposes, which are veiled in the most cryptic of dreams.

This will all be confirmed as person after person listens to you in amazement with astonished looks on their faces. They thank you profusely. You're their hero! You've just interpreted a dream they have been struggling with for years! Then, riding high on your new-found confidence, someone will approach you with a dream and . . . absolutely nothing. No insight, zilch, nada. It's as if the gift has been turned off.

This is very frustrating, especially when you have to turn to the person and admit you cannot help them. I am telling you, if you are in this ministry long enough, your day is coming. Just prepare for it. I cannot help but wonder if times like these are little tests from the Lord. Are we okay with looking "weak" in our gifting? Do we really believe the gift belongs to the Lord and we are just stewards of it, or do we see this as our gift, and we demand to have full control of it at all times? When God is silent I believe this is a wonderful opportunity to remind ourselves at whose pleasure we serve.

When this happens there is really only one thing we can do. Politely thank the person for sharing their dream with us but inform them that the Lord did not reveal anything to us. Why else might this occur? I can think of a few reasons.

Some dreams are not meant to be interpreted in the season they were given. Some dreams are meant to be interpreted years down the road when the dream's contents match the exact time and place God has foreordained for the dreamer. At that specific time in a moment of doubt, in a moment when the person cries out to God for help, He suddenly reminds them of that powerful dream they had years ago. A dream they've never forgotten.

All of a sudden, the veil drops, the understanding comes forth, and they fall on their face in awe of a sovereign God who has planned their steps decades in advance. You can't put a price on a God moment like that, and how wrong would it be of us to speak revelation into a person's life before its appointed time. I believe the Lord sometimes protects dreams from any interpretation until the time is right.

What if, at any given moment, God wants someone else to interpret a person's dream? Perhaps the Lord wants those two people to connect spiritually because He has plans for their relationship down the road. Maybe He wants to use a dream to bring them together. In that instance the person shares a dream with you and God withholds the meaning because the dream is supposed to be heard by someone else. I'm sure our Lord has other reasons, but that is really His business, not ours.

Our business is to simply share an interpretation when He gives us one and politely close our mouths when He has not. We may be tempted to come up with an interpretation from our own wisdom, even though we don't get a strong sense the Holy Spirit is speaking to us. This is a big mistake. We risk giving a wrong interpretation and this is nothing but spiritual pride in action.

Is our desire to appear "anointed" in our gifts and enjoy the praise of others, or is our desire to be a true servant and only speak when we've heard from the Lord? Besides, do we really think this is the way we'll grow more anointed in our gifts? I seem to remember some verse in scripture about the kind of people who do things for the praise of men. If I remember correctly, their reward is the "praise of men," not an increase in their spiritual endowments. Let us choose the better way.

Withholding an Interpretation

Another issue related to our discussion is knowing how much to share even when we feel confident the Holy Spirit has spoken to us. There may be times when a dream is speaking of issues in the person's life that will be very hard to receive. It may be that the Holy Spirit instructs you to share the gist of the message but not all of the details. This is because the person is not ready to hear the full revelation. It could be you are to share a little more later when the timing is more appropriate.

It could just as easily be the case that someone has a very positive dream regarding some amazing things the Lord plans to do in their life or ministry in the near future. I sometimes get a slight check in my spirit when interpreting these kinds of dreams as well. Sometimes it is simply enough to say, "The Lord has some good plans for you in this area. I believe you'll see success here; you're plowing in the right fields."

The person may not have the character to handle the full ramifications of the dream at the time. To tell them all of the dream's implications at the present time would only fill them with pride or cause them to lose focus on their ministry at hand. We must be sensitive to the voice of the Lord at these times and only reveal what we believe we've been given permission to share.

Finally, we would never want to embarrass anyone. If someone shares a dream with me in a public setting, and the interpretation of that dream is actually correcting that person or contains information that might reveal something unflattering about them, then I provide the interpretation privately. It's quite easy to say something along the lines of, "Wow, that is an interesting dream. I think I might have some insight on that, let's talk one-on-one a little later." Again, the golden rule applies here. We should treat others with dignity and respect, the exact same way we'd want them to treat us.

Reveal and Release

When the Lord grants us an interpretation we need to remind ourselves that this is a message from God to that person. We are not responsible for their obedience or disobedience to the dream's requirements. Some may feel the need to follow up and check on the person who received the dream. There may be a temptation to feel slighted if the dreamer is not following the advice or counsel we gave them. An offended interpreter might say, "I can't believe you've not talked to that person yet. I told you the Lord was speaking in that dream about your duty to confront that person. Why aren't you being obedient?"

We need to remind ourselves that we are not, and can never be, anyone else's personal Holy Spirit, constantly checking up on them to see if they're staying on the straight and narrow. I am busy enough with my own spiritual walk and my family's. I certainly don't feel the need to carry that responsibility for someone else's life.

It is an unhealthy desire to want to control other people's lives. The dream interpretation gift is a prophetic gift, and as such, it has its own unique temptations. One of which is the temptation to control others, to hold revelatory information over people's heads. If we recognize the enemy trying to pull us into that trap, we must repent before the Lord and seek His power to break that stronghold. Our role is to "reveal" a dream's meaning and "release" that person to the Lord. He will do in their lives what He so wills, and our part in the process is over after we give the interpretation.

Increasing Your Prophetic Abilities

As we touched on earlier, there are two parts to dream interpretation. There is the natural component in which we draw upon our extensive knowledge of common dream symbols, archetypes, and other clues. There is also the spiritual component, where we carefully listen for insights about the dream, nuances of meaning, and other details that only the Holy Spirit can show us. Good dream interpretation involves staying sharp in both spheres. In the natural, we grow by hearing lots of dreams, learning to identify patterns, and asking good questions to the dreamer to help peel back the layers of their dream.

The spiritual component stays sharp only by having a fresh and growing relationship with God, day in and day out. As we keep that relationship sacred and growing, we'll not have to do anything at all to improve our gift. Growth in the gift will simply be a by-product of our daily walk with God. As we learn to listen to the still small voice of the Lord for our daily needs, it becomes that much easier to recognize that voice in another's dream.

I will say, as I've mentioned before, that there is another discipline that will pay rich dividends in dream interpretation. That is the study of God's Word. So many times when God speaks to people in dreams, He is highlighting biblical truths to them in fresh ways. So often when I'm hearing a dream, my mind is immediately drawn to a scripture verse that perfectly matches the main message of the dream.

The dreamer is often very encouraged to realize that God is giving them a special "mini-movie" highlighting a particular biblical promise just for them. Many times the biblical verse in question even helps me to interpret the overall dream as I see the pieces beginning to fall in place between the verse and specific scenes in the dream. The only way I can pick up on these scriptural insights is by knowing the biblical stories and passages well enough in my heart to recognize them in coded form.

Therefore, if we as dream interpreters wish to grow in our abilities, we must commit to continual growth in our own spiritual lives. We must commit to reading God's Word regularly with the goal of mastering its rich parables, life lessons, and stories of faith. These are literally the "things dreams are made of" when it comes to spiritual dreams.

Submission to Spiritual Authority

I believe we thrive, and so do our gifts, when we are in proper relationships blessed by God. This also includes our spiritual relationships, and I'm specifically speaking about the spiritual authorities God has placed over us. I would be reticent to receive any ministry or any interpretation of my dreams from someone who was not submitted to some spiritual authority in his or her life.

When we are properly submitted to spiritual authority God uses these people to speak blessing, correction, and impartation into our lives. Paul reminds us in Romans 13:1 *"Everyone must submit himself to the governing authorities."* While the context of this verse emphasizes governmental authority, the principle is the same.

Besides, verses such as Hebrew 13:17 explicitly apply this same principle to church leaders.

There are too many unaccountable prophets, dream interpreters, and others running to and fro in churches attempting to speak into the lives of God's people when they themselves have no authority speaking into their own lives. This is not only unbiblical, it's a recipe for abuse. So what authority should dream interpreters be submitted to? It should be a Bible-believing pastor in a solid, local church. Wherever the Lord has placed you, stay submitted to your spiritual shepherd for this is pleasing in God's sight.

In summary, let us make sure we are properly covered and accountable for any ministry that we embark upon. By doing this, we invite God's blessing into our life, and we sharpen the gifts of God within us.

Chapter 10

Case Studies: 7 Dreams Decoded

IT IS NOW TIME to put into practice the truths and principles we have learned. Even if the Lord has not called you to a ministry of dream interpretation, I still believe you'll find the following to be a fun exercise. Below are seven actual dreams I have interpreted over the years. I wish to share them with you and invite you to offer a possible interpretation of them before reading my interpretation.

Remember, if God has given you a gift for interpreting dreams, the gift must be exercised in order to mature. This means you will need a lot of practice and exposure to dreams so you can develop your gift. Sometimes your interpretations will be spot on and sometimes they'll be off. Don't be discouraged. No one gets it right every time. If the dreamer gave me additional comments about the dream, such as how they felt at key moments, I will be sure to include that.

Sometimes I did not get that information because the dream was sent to me in writing and I had no opportunity to ask the dreamer any probing questions. For easy reference, I titled these dreams, and in some cases, I changed the name to protect the identity of the dreamer. Remember to read the dream over carefully and meditate on it asking God to give you insight. If offered, consider the comments and emotions the dreamer shared. Then, reduce the dream to its simplest form, look for any metaphorical images or devices that might be hiding in the dream, scan for any common symbols, and then venture an opinion as to what this dream could mean.

Dream: The Church of Murky Waters

Dreamer: Rebecca

Background: Rebecca and her husband faithfully served as associate pastors at a church until her husband was suddenly asked to resign. Things were going well at the church, and there were no moral or doctrinal issues related to him being asked to step down. After this incident the leadership of the church made no attempt to provide comfort, ignoring them instead.

As this couple worked through their pain and the questioning of why this had happened, Rebecca had the following dream. When I read this dream over, I had to caution her that when we've been hurt by someone, we often cannot trust a negative dream that follows. However, sometimes when we go through a very painful time in our lives, the Lord will give us a dream to help us understand what just transpired.

I often dismiss dreams like this when I know their origins, and I'll often tell people that I do not believe the dream is from God. With this dream, I did sense it was a dream from the Lord given to provide Rebecca with prophetic insight into this church and its leadership.

Rebecca's dream: In my dream I am in my church, leaving a worship service. Everyone is feeling downcast, as if we've all just been reprimanded. I have a sense that this is not even our church building, and we've been tricked by the pastor. As I continue my exit from the service, I keep finding wrapped candy all around the church, so I gather it.

I stop by the ladies room where I see the wife of one of our elders. She is struggling to keep her teeth in her mouth, and so I try to help her. My teeth begin to fall out, and we try to exchange them. I then see another church member, a mother, standing in an open stall dyeing her hair with multicolored dye. Her child is standing in the toilet, and the mother is oblivious. I feel responsible to clean the child but have no ill feelings for the mother.

Finally, I walk into the church hallway where I see three scuba divers emerging from murky waters that are waist deep in another hall. I wake up strangely peaceful and certain that I must pray for this church and the body of Christ.

My interpretation: This dream is a revelatory dream providing you with a report on the spiritual state of this church and its leadership. The entire dream is filled with negative imagery, so we immediately know much about this church's current state of spiritual health.

The feeling of being tricked about what building you are worshipping in denotes that you don't trust this pastor or what he says, even in such a simple matter as where you physically are. You mentioned that, after the worship service, people walked out feeling downcast. This reflects the overall mood or emotional health of the members. Leaving a worship service where one has just worshipped the living God should leave us excited and full of hope, not downcast. Many of the members are not experiencing this grace in their lives at the present time.

In the dream, you are the only one who notices the wrapped candy lying around, meaning you are the one who can see potential, the evidences of God's sweet little graces that heretofore have been unnoticed by the leadership because they are undiscerning. The woman in the bathroom is dyeing her hair, an activity which should not be occurring in a church. It is a worldly (though not "sinful") activity taking place in a consecrated, spiritual environment. It is a barometer of the spiritual health of this church. Some of the members are not concerned with Kingdom things, but rather with the insignificant affairs of their everyday world. This is because the leadership has failed to teach them.

The mother, whose daughter was found in the toilet—a very unsanitary place—is left unattended, signifying that this mindset is affecting the younger generation as well. The lack of spiritual maturity in the members means the children won't receive proper instruction and care from their parents.

Walking into the hallways and seeing three scuba divers coming out of murky waters shows that foreign influences (spiritual) are in the church and are roaming at will, unchecked and unchallenged by the leadership. The leadership does not know who or what roams their halls. This is obviously not a positive dream. Pray for the church, its leaders, and its members. God lead you in all things.

Final thoughts: In its simplest form, this dream is a series of vignettes in which Rebecca walks the perimeter of the church and upon each "station," encounters evidences of spiritual apathy. There is a descending progression in this theme beginning with: 1) the church leadership, which is very visible in the community, 2) the church membership, which is somewhat visible, and 3) the unseen world of spiritual forces (the scuba divers), which are completely invisible.

As Rebecca leaves the sanctuary, she finds wrapped candy (God's sweet little graces). Although lying in plain sight, they have not been noticed by the leadership. This points to a lack of discernment on their part. They don't "see" spiritual things that should be obvious.

She then stops by the restroom where the manifestation of the church's leadership level is shown in the life of its members. Sharp, spiritually skilled leadership produces spiritually quick Christians. In this church, the people are simply rising to the level of their leaders, and that level is nothing to boast about. The woman dyeing her hair in the church bathroom is a symbolic portrait of carnal, common things occurring in a spiritual environment. It's simply a type of activity representing *all* non-spiritual activities.

Losing teeth can sometimes symbolize losing wisdom and sometimes can, among other things, symbolize losing power. In this instance, I believe it symbolizes both—leadership that is neither wise nor powerful in spiritual matters. The elder's wife represents all the elders in the church. Rebecca's teeth falling out represent her sense of impotence to face the insurmountable challenges facing this church and her powerlessness to exert influence over the congregation due to their loss of position.

Finally, finding water in a church is not unusual because water represents the Holy Spirit, but this water is murky and contaminated. The divers arise out of a spiritual thing (water) because they are spiritual beings (demonic influences). They must don scuba gear to walk the halls of the church because, as demonic forces, a church is a foreign environment to them. They are "out of their element" and require special gear (special permission) to operate there. They then walk to and fro throughout the church, signifying their partial habitation there, where they wield at least some level of influence.

Dream: Dual Lights in the Night

Dreamer: Robert

Robert's dream: I dreamed I was at a large party at a huge mansion. The party was being held outdoors at night. Bright lights stationed all around the mansion were shining light to the ground, so people could see. There were over a hundred people in groups of three to six, each standing around talking.

I looked up in the night sky and noticed a spot of light beginning to open in the distant dark clouds. One of the bright white clouds took on the shape of a lamb. Other turbulent clouds boiled and swirled around the lamb.

My mom was sitting on the porch of a neighboring house. I yelled to her to look at the bright display in the night sky. She was a long distance away and I wasn't sure that she heard me, so I shouted again for her to look. She motioned to me that she was watching.

I looked back to the sky. The white lamb stood stationary in the sky while the clouds swirling around it took on the form of winged, heavenly beings. The scene in the sky grew in size as more dark clouds became bright and turned into angels. I began to hear music coming from the sky. The angels were singing.

I wanted to continue watching this awesome spectacle, but I had an overwhelming urge to tell everyone else at the party what was going on in the heavens, so they could see it too. I turned to look at the people. Some were already looking at the sky. Either they had noticed it themselves or had heard me yelling to my mom about it. I walked to each group of people who were not looking up and urged them to gaze upon the glorious scene in the sky.

Many people I spoke to did look up. As they did, the bright lights from the mansion interfered with their view. Some held up their hands to block the house lights. I thought to myself, I have to find a way to turn these flood lights off so everyone can see the dramatic show in the sky. Just as I started to walk toward the door to the mansion, I woke up.

The experience had been very exciting and my heart was pounding. What could this dream mean and why did I have it?

My interpretation: This is an encouragement/revelatory dream and the meaning is clear. In essence, this dream points to the fact that there exists as of now, two worlds: one natural (the party/social scene on earth) and one supernatural (symbolized by the heavenly manifestations). Most people are unaware of the real world of God's Kingdom as demonstrated by the partygoers talking and taking absolutely no notice of the heavenly display swirling wildly right above them. You, and all Christians for that matter, are called out of this world and are sensitive to the priorities of the Kingdom. These called out ones, the church, have a mission to help others "see the light" as you were doing in your dream.

In this evangelistic endeavor to which you are called, you will have mixed success, even as did the apostle Paul in Acts 17:16–34. Some will mock you and not look to the lights, some will "consider" what you say about the lights, but some will believe you and be saved (see vv. 32–34). The lights of this world (the house lights at the mansion) block out the lights of the Spirit making it difficult to comprehend, appreciate, or to even see the glory of God and His lights. These house lights represent the cares of the world, sin, ignorance, etc.

Your mission is two fold: tell them about the lights through witnessing and preaching but also remove the distractions (turn off the house lights) by praying and interceding for obstacles of the gospel to be removed. This may sometimes involve you actually doing physical things or getting involved in ministry projects which lead to action. You are both to *speak* and *act* to help people see the lights.

May God give you insight into what to do and when to do it. The dark clouds turning white and morphing into angels speaks of the inevitability of the Kingdom of God to be victorious over the kingdom of the evil one. God is literally taking ground from the enemy and transforming it into ground for the Kingdom of God! This is a very encouraging dream. You are part of God's army to bring others to the light of the glorious gospel of Christ. Since you are called, you will also be equipped.

Final thoughts: I love the rich symbolism God gave Robert in this dream. How appropriate that God used light, which represents illumination, to show us in picture form that too much natural light overloads our eyes, so we cannot see the spiritual light from above.

Reduced to its simplest form, this dream is about competing lights and one man's attempt to get people to become aware of the more significant, heavenly light. Everything else is just details supporting the main thrust of the dream, which is: *without a herald, people in their natural state will never see the greater light*. Did you notice the expression of helping people "see the light" that showed up in this dream? That metaphor serves as the interpretative key that unlocks the dream's meaning. As I've mentioned to you, always look for metaphors, idioms, and word plays. They are extremely common in dreams and will often lead you to the dream's meaning.

You'll notice I made no comment about Robert's mention of his mother. Could there have been some significance to her making a cameo in the dream? Possibly. I simply didn't get anything from that scene, so I ignored it, not feeling it relevant to the dream's overall message. I do not feel any pressure or need to comment on every character, item, or statement made in any given dream.

Sometimes these are simply filler material that get lumped into a spiritual dream, perhaps from one's subconscious; or, again, they could be additional, helpful insights but simply go un-coded by the interpreter. We must simply do our best on a case-by case basis to provide insight on the symbols we do understand and leave what remains to the dreamer to do with as he will.

Dream: The Hiding Place

Dreamer: Rachel

Rachel's dream: I am a mother, a wife, and a student at a Baptist university. When I was in my mid-twenties, I had a dream I have always wondered about. I still to this day remember everything about that dream. This is strange because usually I'm lucky if I can remember a dream from the night before, let alone a dream from years ago. I would love to get your opinion on what you think it means.

The dream starts out with me in a city I've never seen or been to. I'm walking on the sidewalk with other people who are on their way to work or whatever. For some reason I look up and there are black clouds rolling in fast, but they are not rain clouds, they are something more. As I look around, there happens to be a dirt road that leads into the city, and on this road, traveling to the city, are emergency vehicles. Right around this time, other people see the vehicles and of course begin to panic.

They begin running to any kind of shelter they can find. As they are running, I see ugly, hideous, mean demons chasing and eating people. I run into the alley to hide, and I find a little room where others are hiding. They call me over and open the door to let me hide with them. The room is filled with other people who are obviously scared and hoping not to be caught by the demons.

We can see outside that the demons are everywhere eating people, but we are safe. I now notice an angel standing nearby our hiding place. I'm not sure when she appeared. She could have been there the whole time, or I could have just noticed her. She is just standing outside of our hiding place, arms crossed, and looking on.

Then, I see an old man run into our alley. The old man is being chased by a demon. The old man looks at me, and I want to let him in, but the others will not let me because they say there is no room, and they do not want to draw attention to themselves. We all start arguing. I look and the demon has caught up with him and is attacking him. The angel is still outside, still watching, but doing nothing. As I'm watching, I decide to help, which is suicide because this is a hopeless battle, and I know I won't win, but I just can't watch this poor man being eaten.

All of a sudden, after I decide to help him, I feel the most amazing love for this old man that I've felt for anything or anyone. I actually felt this in the dream. This part was a gift because I have never felt like that, ever. The demon steps back like he is getting a better look at his kill. I know what is coming, so I put my body over the old man's to protect him. Then, amazingly, this is when the angel steps up and fights the demon and kills him. That is the end of the dream.

My interpretation: This is a revelatory/spiritual warfare dream. The dark rolling clouds advancing toward the city represents the kingdom forces of the enemy encroaching upon the earth. This is a picture of the great spiritual war between the Kingdom of God and the kingdom of evil. A dirt road represents that entrance into this earthly kingdom is temporary and inferior to the Kingdom of God, where the very streets are made of gold (Revelation 21:21).

The city represents the entire earth, not just one city. The demons attack mankind at will (II Timothy 2:26, I Peter 5:8). The ambulances roaring into the city symbolize the utter futility of using government, man-made solutions to tackle spiritual problems. The effects of sin, and the attack of the enemy, can't be helped, no matter how many ambulances, SWAT teams, or anything else runs to assist. They will all turn back, overwhelmed by the power of the demons.

You hiding represents the fact that some Christians, out of fear or indifference, seek to stay on the side lines in this great spiritual war, resting content that, "Thank God we're saved! I'm glad I'm not a part of this evil generation who are getting attacked by Satan's forces." They can have such an attitude, and they will be relatively protected by nature of their relationship with God. They were protected were they not, by the mighty angel? However, God is looking for a different kind of Christian in today's battle.

He's looking for Christians who will not only keep themselves unspotted from the world, but will also take an active part in combat during this war. He's looking for the kind who are willing to leave the security of their groups and churches and who will go out to save others from their own destruction. As you stepped out in sacrificial love and ministry, you caught a glimpse of the heart of God (for a moment you felt how He feels for sinners), and you were willing to die if necessary, to save others.

As you stepped out, God's power, protection, and provision went with you because you were on a mission for Him. God's power and provision were symbolized by the angel following you and fighting the enemy. When your faith was released to act, the power of God was released to move! The man was saved.

The dream ends, not with an outright victory for this city, but with a victory in this one battle. This is because it is not for us to know the times and seasons of our Lord's return. It is however, enough for us to know that in our circle of influence, when we call out for His power and move out to minister in His name, He is with us in the battle. This is a very positive dream. May you go out and be an active participant in the Kingdom of God, saving as many as you can, using every possible means before it's too late.

Final thoughts: It is not uncommon for dark rolling clouds or other hazardous weather patterns (cyclones, tornados, etc.) to serve as omens of danger or spiritual warfare. This makes sense when we consider that these storms occur "in the heavens" and thus sometimes represent heavenly battles or trials.

When we examine the emotions of this dream, we see two distinct patterns. We see those of the people versus those of Rachel. In the dream, the crowd in hiding reveals emotions of fear and self-preservation. Rachel, however, reveals emotions of courage and self-sacrifice. Therefore, we know the dream is dark because of the predominant feeling of fear and terror pervading the story, but we know that this is a dark story with a positive message at the end. The message of this dream is: when we act in faith, God shows up and has our back.

Dream: Welcome to Your New World

Dreamer: Kim

Kim's dream: I had a dream that I was travelling to a new city. The old world had been destroyed. On this journey I had a companion with me. We arrived at this "new world" by descending from the sky and I noticed that everything was made of light and crystal. It had a very "space age" look.

All I remember about the old world was that it had been completely obliterated, sort of like through an explosion. I remember thinking it was strange that I was not sad about this. As we arrived, we went to some registration area that looked like a railway station. There were helpers there ready to assist us. We went to find out if we could get a house. We needed to live somewhere since we were new here. The workers said, "sure." They didn't blink an eye and immediately said, "We've got yours assigned." They handed us keys to our new homes.

The transportation system used to get us to our new homes was some kind of silver pods which travelled through big, clear pneumatic tubes. We were carried away through the tubes over to our new home. They were all in a row-like townhouses. On the inside of the houses there were no walls dividing the residences. All had separate doors on the outside but no walls internally once you entered the master unit. Furniture was haphazardly set up, kind of like in a furniture store display setting, just pieces placed here and there.

Two men, one white with dark hair, the other black, came to welcome me. They were neighbors and had entered from their houses within the overall housing unit (they came into my home from the inside not the outside). My companion had been housed next to me. He was checking out his new home. I then saw him and asked if he would stay with me and sleep in the bed with me since it was our first night in this new place. Initially, I didn't have romantic feelings for him at all, but it seemed as though I was beginning to have strong feelings for this man. I then noticed that there were some people shopping for house stuff at a store connected at the end of the row of houses.

My interpretation: This is an encouragement/prophetic dream. I believe God is showing you what he has recently done for you and what He will continue doing for you in the near future. The dream portrays God in the process of reengineering your social/support network of friends, trusted companions, and ultimately your life partner.

The "old world" in this dream represents exactly that—your "old world." God is doing something new and wonderful in you, and if you'll stay submitted to His will for your life, I think you have some very good times ahead of you in the area of relationships. I believe this dream is speaking of new friends, new realms, a new community, and new opportunities God has in store for you. He is opening a "new world" to you.

Your arrival to this new world is from above, signifying that the travel agent on this trip came from above, i.e. from heaven. You arrived at your new community via a silver vehicle that travelled through clear tubes. In biblical literature, silver speaks of redemption. Traveling through clear tubes represents transparency. Your new relationships will be marked by grace and transparency. This will be the currency of the new relationships God is bringing into your life.

The fact that each inhabitant has their own private entrance but there are no internal walls once inside the super-structure speaks to a close-knit, grace-centered community where everyone is their brother's and sister's keepers. Access to the inner lives of the community is easy because "walls" have been torn down.

The incomplete furniture layout represents a life, a calling that is incomplete. The steps are not all there at the present. You will, on this new journey with Christ, gradually put within your home the things you need to live your life for Him. He will add to your home (your life) the tools, furnishings, and décor tailor made for you! I also believe the companion in your dream indicates that, in due time, this journey of yours is not meant to be lived by you alone. God will send you a helpmate who will go on this exciting journey with you.

Final thoughts: Notice that this dream incorporates a number of common dream symbols. We have the vehicle (silver pods) representing the new direction Kim's life is taking. We have the color silver encoded in the dream, and in this instance, it takes on its most common meaning, that of grace and redemption. Traveling in clear tubes does represent transparency, but in this case, it's a double symbol representing that the transparency results from a work of the Spirit. Invisible or see-through people or objects often denote unseen spiritual forces, either the Holy Spirit or the unseen world of the enemy.

We also see the common house symbol appear. What stands out in this house dream is that these homes are arranged very tightly together. Kim described them as townhomes. Our attention is immediately drawn to the fact that these homes have no walls. What do walls do? Negatively, walls are used in our culture to speak of erecting protective defenses in our life when we don't wish to allow others into our inner world. We often say, "I can't speak to Bob about this, he's put a wall up with me." Positively, walls allow us a measure of privacy as when we go behind closed doors.

In the dream, Kim didn't feel threatened or frustrated when the two men suddenly appeared to pay her a visit. Here, we allow Kim's own feelings in the dream to help us decode the meaning of these symbols. Her reaction to the two men signifies to us that the missing walls in this dream are not a bad thing, they serve a positive function. That is, they allow this community to be tight-knit and transparent.

Each person has their own private home, so this is not some kind of communal cult where people lose their identities, but this new community is characterized by an openness that is sadly growing increasingly uncommon in our culture.

Dream: The Black Rider

Dreamer: Erica

Erica's dream: I dreamed I was outside late at night, and I looked up at the sky and saw something coming down from above. I realized it was a man in all black, riding on a horse. As he was descending he passed in front of the moon, and I saw his silhouette. It reminded me of that famous scene in the movie *E.T.* where the boys were all riding their bicycles and began floating in the air. When they passed in front of the moon you could see their outlines passing by.

As the dark figure was approaching, I saw my sister sleeping just a few feet away from me. The dark rider made it down to where we were and looked me right in the eye, but I had no fear. I sensed he was on a mission. He then galloped away. During all of this, my sister, still half asleep, must have heard some of this because she then said groggily, "It's the 8:53 train." I then woke up. I didn't think this rider was evil but was sent to my sister for a specific reason. I had the sense that it was a rider of poverty or famine.

My interpretation: Erica, I believe this is a warning dream. Because you felt no fear from this dark rider, and you yourself said you did not feel it was an evil rider, I will defer to your judgment in the matter. I believe this is a messenger of judgment, and the message is that very soon your sister will go through a dark time of penalty or judgment because of some circumstances she is involved in.

The rider comes from the sky signifying that he is a spiritual messenger. The fact that your sister is asleep during all of this points to the fact that, at the present, she is "unaware" of the situation brewing around her which is beckoning the dark rider. When the rider does appear she does not ascribe to him his proper identity, as an instrument of divine judgment, but rather she thinks she hears a train coming, which will simply take her to some destination of her choosing. Her groggy state, coupled with the train comment, is a double-reinforced symbol indicating that she does not see this "train coming down the track" (i.e., the consequences of her present course).

Final thoughts: Do you notice that once again an idiom, in this case, "doesn't see that train coming down the track," helps us to interpret this dream? That idiom reveals that when this judgment occurs, it will take this woman completely off guard. Something bad will soon happen to her, and right up until the last moment, she will not see it coming.

The rider dressed in all black is not a good symbol either. Black usually signifies sin, judgment, or a bad omen. In this instance the color of the rider denotes the content of his message (judgment), not his origin (heaven). A rider coming from the sky represents that this judgment originates from above, although the actual manifestation of judgment will take place on the earth.

Did you also notice the time mentioned in the dream? 8:53. 8:53 is "almost" nine o'clock. The number nine can sometimes represent judgment. So the dream, in essence, is revealing that a time of judgment is "almost" here. Since the time of judgment is seven minutes till nine, the seven signifies that the judgment is from God (seven is God's number). So, we see that this dream displays a double-reinforced message pointing toward judgment: 1) the rider is dressed in all black and black often denotes judgment, and 2) the time is almost nine o'clock, and nine is the number of judgment.

Also, note that in this dream the horse is associated with judgment. Horses usually don't symbolize judgment (usually it's bears) but the Holy Spirit told me in this dream the horse did symbolize judgement. This is why we can't say those common symbols have a 100% fixed meaning. Dream interpretation is fluid and absolutely requires the anointing of the Holy Spirit each and every time we interpret a dream. Don't depend on formulas.

Before, during, and after this dream, Erica had a growing sense that something just was not right with her sister. The family was concerned but nothing they did was helping because this family member would not open up about what was going on in her life. Unfortunately, about six months after this dream occurred her actions caught up with her. Erica's sister was arrested and the family finally learned that she had been involved in some illegal activities.

The sister went on to serve a significant prison term. Erica's initial assessment of the dark rider as a judgment of poverty or famine was also accurate. In prison you have no luxuries, no personal property to speak of, and it is in many ways a long season of actual and spiritual poverty and famine.

Dream: Your New Home Awaits You

Dreamer: Amber

Amber's dream: I dreamed that I was in the market for a new house. There were two houses I wanted to view. The one I really wanted appeared small from the outside, but I knew that once inside it was really much larger. The couple that was showing me the house was an actual couple I know. It was their home.

I arrived at the house along with my mother and daughter. The first thing I noticed was the homeowner's husband just sitting on the couch watching T.V. I then looked off to my left and saw that the living room had a huge stage and platform built into it. It looked like some sort of concert hall. It was nicely decked out with everything one would need to speak or perform.

I remember thinking that I very much wanted to see the bedroom. I was very drawn to it, so I had her take me there next. When she opened the door to the bedroom, I was in awe. It was huge with marble floors, gold columns and pillars supporting the ceiling, and just beautiful to look upon. I didn't see much furniture in the room though.

The woman walked me down a hall, and as I looked off, I saw a large room similar to a banquet hall. There were lots of tables and chairs in that room. I remember thinking that this room didn't quite match the rest of the home so far. The house didn't seem like it quite "fit" in terms of style and architecture, but I didn't mind because, so far, I was really impressed with this house. It was then that I noticed a lot of other people crowding in the hallways trying to speak to the woman. I thought to myself, "There are a

Decoding Your Spiritual Dreams

lot of people who want this house. I'm going to have to put a bid in quickly."

Then the woman showed me the last section of the house. This part of the house was not very fancy like all the other rooms. In fact, it was a series of rooms lined up down a hallway. The doors to these rooms had old cracked paint, which was beginning to peel off. The woman told me that these rooms had rented tenants, and they came with the house. I knocked on one of the doors and an old man peered out to look at me, and then, after a few moments, he shut the door. I decided that I still wanted this house, even if it came with those old rooms and tenants.

I asked the woman how much this house cost. I was expecting a very large amount, but to my surprise, she told me it was selling for $90,000. I thought about it and realized that my payments would be in the $700 range, and I could afford it. That was the end of the dream.

My interpretation: Amber, I got a very good feeling about this dream as I prayed over it. I believe this is a prophetic dream revealing the future size and scope of your life and ministry. The fact the house appears to be small but intuitively you knew it to actually be larger points to the fact that God has plans to greatly enlarge your territory in the future.

Your "living" room points to the fact that some of what you and your husband will do for a "living" will involve ministry that is very visible. That is, ministry that takes place on stages. This can involve speaking, singing, and other ministry taking place in the context of large crowds.

When you looked at your bedroom, you noticed the opulent décor of the marble floors and gold pillars. This speaks of the intimacy that God wants with you. The intimate parts of your walk with God (the bedroom of your house) will be characterized by beauty and grandeur. When you saw your dining room area you rightly described it as a banquet hall. It had many tables and chairs which represents the fact that you will break bread and fellowship with thousands of people. A normal dining room will have a table with 6 or 8 chairs. Your dining room table and chairs represents the large numbers of people who will come in and out of your life due to the influence and visibility you and your husband will share.

The fact that large numbers of people were crowding into your house and wanting the home for themselves signifies that you will have to deal with issues of jealously at some point over your life and ministry. There will be other Christians who will be envious of you. They want your life (your home) because of its benefits and privileges. You will have to ask God for grace, kindness, and sensitivity as you deal with this down the road. Do not be tempted to retaliate, but instead, shower others with love in a spirit of Christ-likeness.

Overall, this dream is very positive, but I did get a negative sense regarding one of the scenes. You mentioned that one part of the house contained some old tenants, and their area of the house was not in good repair (signified by the cracked paint and old look). I think this symbol has two meanings, one positive, the other negative.

On the positive side, I believe your ministry will include a mix of cutting edge power in the Spirit but also some very fundamental, traditional, no-frill aspects, such as mercy ministries to the elderly, oppressed, or downtrodden. This is in stark contrast to the flashier, power-encounter based platform ministries represented by the stage in the living room. In many ways your life and ministry will be a mixture of some parts powerful, and for lack of a better word "sensational," while other parts will be very traditional and won't attract much attention.

On the negative side, I believe the old tenants represent parts of your "old man" (flesh) that are moving into this house with you. Even though God wants to do some amazing things in your life and ministry, there will be the same old problems, issues, and insecurities to deal with even in this future season. These issues are compartmentalized as old rooms appearing in your otherwise very impressive new home. We never are totally free from that old man, but as we continue our walk of faith, the Lord brings us to new levels of deliverance as we move from glory to glory. He'll do the same with you.

You stated that the house didn't seem to "fit" quite right. I too got the same sense but felt no negativity from this. I believe this is because, in many ways, the ministry you and your husband will have will not be traditional. I see a mixture of very traditional ministry operating smoothly alongside very cutting edge, avant-garde ministry.

It is not a coincidence that the price of the home was listed as $90,000. In biblical literature, nine can have several meanings, not least of which is the idea of "divine completion" or "fullness." 90,000 is just an exaggeration of 9 (it's like 9 on steroids!). So, when will you get to move into this new house? When God's timing is "complete." Your payment was in the $700s. That too is significant. The number seven in biblical writings is associated with the idea of "perfection" and completion as well. This simply means that the payments needed to obtain this new home will come as you walk in Christ's "perfect" will for your life. As you do this day by day, year by year, you are making deposits into your future destiny (your future "home"). Matthew 25:21 speaks clearly to this principle.

Overall, this is a very positive dream portraying the size and scope of the ministry God intends for your family down the road. May our Lord give you His grace and blessings as you continue to serve Him.

Final thoughts: Here we see the common house theme make another appearance. While this house definitely portrays aspects of herself, I received a strong impression that the house also represented Amber's ministry. This is an example of just listening to the Holy Spirit and picking up on nuances of meaning that may be added even to common symbols. The platform living room and the large table and chairs do indeed represent people and experiences that will be occurring within Amber's life, but many of these occurrences will take place in the context of her ministry.

Let us consider another scene in the dream that appears neutral on the surface. After viewing the dining room with the tables and chairs, Amber sees numerous people attempting to get to the homeowner because they too want to purchase the house. She made no mention to me of feeling threatened, nor was there any mention of these people being rude, jealous, or bad.

However, as I considered the dream my spirit was quickened to this symbol and I felt intuitively that it was negative. What immediately came to me was that these people were jealous and wanted the house for themselves. Again, this reminds us that in dream interpretation, some symbols and scenes are fairly obvious, while others could have many logical interpretations, some negative, some positive, and some neutral.

How then do we interpret the dream correctly? We do this by relying on God's Holy Spirit to reveal to us the meaning of cryptic or open-ended scenes and symbols. Always remember the #1 rule of dream interpretation: dream interpretations come from God.

Dream: The Spiritual World Series

Dreamer: Michael

Background: This dream comes from a believer who receives spiritual dreams quite frequently. The Lord often gives Michael prophetic dreams that speak to the corporate church at large. Let me also add some additional background information, which will be helpful.

Michael loves baseball, and in his youth he was part of a little league team that was extraordinarily talented. Their coach, who I'll call "Mr. Trevino," was somewhat of a local hero around their community having coached this team to several championships. Michael has great respect for coach Trevino. In Michael's dreams, the game of baseball often represents the work of the ministry. A major thrust of Michael's ministry is his desire to see personal and corporate revival in the church. This is a theme he speaks on often when he ministers publically in churches.

I will also note that Michael grew up in Vineland, New Jersey. Vineland was the origin of a great revival that took place in 1867. During this outpouring, thousands of people came to Christ, and many were healed and set free from bondages as the Spirit moved through these meetings. The Vineland meetings were in some ways a forerunner of the later 1906 Azusa Street Revival, which was the birthplace of the modern Pentecostal/charismatic movement.

Some of the leaders of the Azusa Street revival were influenced by those who attended the Vineland meetings. The baseball field where Michael would play as a child was the same field where many of these meetings took place. In fact, still today there lays a memorial stone in this field with the simple inscription, "National Holiness Association 1867–1967."

Michael's dream: In my dream, I am a member of a baseball team, and we are playing in a big game. My team is made up of members of mediocre talent. They are not that great at catching, throwing the ball accurately, or anything else. Some are not very good at all. I have pretty good baseball skills, but I know that my abilities alone cannot carry this team to victory. In the dream, I care a great deal about these guys, and I want to help them win. For some reason, we don't have a coach, but I know that I and one other player are the captains. We will have to lead this team somehow.

The other team is highly skilled. They are excellent runners and batters and are all around very well-conditioned athletes. They are coached by coach Trevino, my old little league coach, so this makes them even more formidable than they already are. If that were not enough, this team is invisible, so it is very hard to play against them because we can't even see their movements on the field. I remember that I didn't fear this team. Their invisibility didn't make them bad or anything. I actually remember respecting them, just being in awe at how well they played.

We began playing the game, and of course, they were beating us. Our guys just could not match their level of play. I remember that it was the beginning of the 7th inning, and I was the first up to bat. They had 9 points and we had 3. I remember thinking that if I could hit a home run and help us score some runs, maybe we had a chance against them, especially if the guys who came after me also did well. It was a long shot, but I still had hope that we might somehow pull off an upset.

As I walked toward the plate, getting ready to bat, the umpire called the game and it was all over. I remember thinking to myself,

"I can't believe he called this game." I was frustrated, but I eventually accepted his ruling and made my way off the field. Then I looked up and I noticed the call box that was high above the field. It sat just behind and above the chain link fence that encircled the field. I began to climb the fence and eventually I made it to the top where I peered my head over and looked into the call box.

There, I saw all of my teammates sitting at tables and eating and talking. They did not seem too upset that we had lost the game, or that we had the game called early, or that even if we had been allowed to play it out that we would probably have lost. They were content to just eat and fellowship among themselves. I decided that I too would eat something. I found myself eating on the floor next to one of their tables. There were no other chairs left in the hall.

Then I saw coach Trevino's wife, so I made my way over to her. It was great seeing her after all of these years and I asked her how she was doing. She told me that she and coach Trevino had divorced. I asked her why they divorced and she said, "He loved baseball more than he loved me." Then I woke up.

My interpretation: This is a revelatory dream depicting two generations of revivalists and leaders who are playing a heavenly exhibition match representing how both teams "played the game" in their prime. The one team is the generation of 1867 who I'll call "The Invisibles," and the other team is the generation of 2010 who I'll call "The Moderns."

The Moderns have some skills, and they are able to put up some points against the other team, but ultimately it's no comparison. The Invisibles still outscored the Moderns 3 to 1. The fact that your team does not have a coach, and you end up having to, in effect, coach the team yourself points to a spiritual disappointment in your own life.

I believe you may have longed for mentors in your life who would have taught you the deeper things of the Spirit. I believe the Lord has brought some men into your life that served this purpose to an extent but not at the level you've really desired. In many ways, you find yourself influencing and leading people from your own generation, but you still wish you had been better equipped for that task by having had long-term mentors of your own.

The Invisibles are, in many ways, superior in the things of the Spirit when compared to this generation of revivalists and leaders. They were the better coached team. I believe this signifies that the older generation did a better job of developing their promising "players." They created a farm team, nurtured and coached the talent, and those players went on to the big leagues where they became forces to be reckoned with.

The fact that they were invisible has two meanings. On one level, because they are so closely associated with a powerful move of the Spirit, who is invisible, they too are invisible as they take on the form of their source. On another level, this team from 1867 is invisible because, quite frankly—they're dead. Their successes and failures, their faith journey in the Spirit, both the victories and the setbacks, are all now in the past, time locked, sealed, and final.

In a very real sense, you cannot "play" a game alongside them today. They had their day and had their chance. They are, in today's world, invisible and irrelevant in some sense. Today's ministry, today's godless generation, will not be able to be influenced by the team from 1867. All that the world of today will have to meet their needs is the team of 2010.

The game was called early because this current generation does not have the discipline and stamina to compete in a long game. Had the game been allowed to continue, the disparity in the score would have continued to run up in favor of the Invisibles. In effect, the umpire (God) invoked the mercy rule and called the game.

When you climbed the fence to look into the box, you were seeking to get God's perspective on how this game was played. The call box is where the professionals who know how the game is played make their judgments on how it all turned out. The call box is where God and the heavenly cloud of witnesses (former players themselves) watch these new games. These professionals know the players, their backgrounds, the rules of the game, and they have a sense of history of how this game has been played by different teams over the years.

Your current team will one day be there too (as symbolized by seeing them now in the call box, joining their predecessors). You are being given a glimpse of their attitude. They do not have the same competitive drive that you do. This is signified by them eating and talking. The fact that they were playing the game so poorly compared to the team from 1867 didn't disturb them as badly as it disturbed you. You didn't eat next to them at the table because, in some ways, you are not of their ilk, even though you played the game at the same time they did. You not being at the table with them signifies that you are not totally associated with them.

When you spoke to coach Trevino's wife, her answer was very significant for it is the key to why the team from 1867 were so good. On the surface, her pronouncement of a dissolved marriage may seem like a bad, negative thing, but it is not. We must remember that in this dream the game of baseball is not the game of baseball. Baseball represents the Kingdom of God and one's level of skill and service in the Kingdom.

To say that her husband left her because he loved baseball more than her is, in effect, saying that many in the generation of 1867 loved Jesus more than anything else, and they were willing to center their entire lives around their allegiance and service to Him. (The Lord is highlighting Luke 14:26 to you through Mrs. Trevino's speech.) The team from 1867 loved Jesus *more,* wanted sin eradicated from their life *more,* and wanted to do what was necessary to win *more* than what today's generation is willing to do.

Let us consider today's events. Can we honestly say that the modern day revivals in America over the last ten or twenty years are comparable to the First or Second Great Awakening? As we compare the two, what do we really see in terms of the spiritual depth of the revivalists leading the movement? What price were the Christians willing to pay in days past as compared to today in order to see revival come? What do we see in terms of societal transformation in the community after the meetings cease?

In our modern era we are the benefactors of such a powerful heritage. We live post-Azusa Street. We understand the gifts of the Spirit and dreams and visions. We have access to powerful biblical teaching and impartation through the abundant resources available on the internet and through books, podcasts, and other media. These advantages, if not coupled with other spiritual disciplines like solitude and simplicity, do us no good.

Those who came before us, while lacking in some things, were far more advanced than we are today. Ponder on these things, and may God give you insight. Ask God to continue to make you an effective leader of men. May we not discount our spiritual forefathers, for in many ways, we are their students still (Proverbs 22:28).

Final thoughts: After I gave Michael this interpretation, his spirit bore witness to it, and he shared with me that this was exactly the interpretation God gave him. He was very excited to see that he now had confirmation on the dream's meaning. However, he shared that God gave him additional insight about the numbers appearing in the dream that I didn't touch on.

You will remember that the game was called by God in the 7th inning, and at the time, the score was 9 to 3. The 7th inning represents completion. God was saying that He temporarily stopped the game, but He will resume it for Michael again one day in the 7th inning of Michael's life (in Michael's time of personal completion or maturity). He then reminded Michael that in his future 7th inning, the cumulative score of the two teams would point to what God wanted to do with this generation if they would cooperate.

Thus, the Modern's score of 3 represented God's fullness, which this generation possesses in some aspects. The Invisible's score of 9 represented completion in the Spirit, which the former generation possessed in some aspects. When the best of the former generation's heart and abilities (9) were added to this generation's fullness of the Spirit (3), the result would be 12. Twelve in biblical literature represents godly governmental rule. God was, in effect, relaying to Michael that a great effectiveness in spiritual authority and rule was coming from this future generation if it would submit to God's refining fire and continued coaching.

Afterword

THE PRINCIPLES SHARED IN this book will take time and practice to master, but the effort will be worth the labor. For those of you who have a history of receiving spiritual dreams, it is my prayer that this study has provided you with a whole new set of tools in which to better interpret these heavenly messages. For those of you who have not had much experience with spiritual dreams, I hope you will ask God in faith to begin speaking to you this way. I believe you will find our Lord will grant that very request, especially when we are quick to obey His biddings.

In both our natural and spiritual dreams we can learn so much about ourselves, our real values, our hopes, and our fears. Rather than discounting these nocturnal revelations, may we instead give them a place of respect in our lives, taking the time in our morning wake to separate the wheat from the chaff.

Few things are more meaningful than intimate communication, received and understood, between a holy God and His people. What an amazing God we serve. A God who takes the time to confirm our deepest questions, to warn of dangers yet unaware, and to whisper His plans into our souls as we've quieted them before Him. For thousands of years God has been speaking this way to His people. For those who have ears to hear, let our response to Him be even as His servant Samuel who also heard His voice in the night and cried:

> *"Speak Lord, for your servant is listening."* (1 Samuel 3:10)

Glossary

Oneirology—The study of dreams. The scientific process of studying the causation and purpose of dreaming.

Intrinsic dream—A dream in which God provides one with insight and instruction about themselves.

Extrinsic dream—A dream in which God provides one with insight and instruction about someone else.

Spiritual dream—A dream given by God to an individual in order to communicate His will regarding a specific matter.

TYPES OF SPIRITUAL DREAMS:

Portrait dream—A dream given by God to an individual to reveal their current level of spiritual, mental, and emotional health.

Confirmation dream—A dream given by God to an individual to confirm the truth about their current thoughts, aspirations, or judgments about a matter.

Encouragement dream—A dream given by God to an individual to remind them of His pleasure, protection, and grace in their life.

Prophetic dream—A dream given by God to an individual regarding something that will occur in the future for the purposes of calling that person to prayer and preparation.

Spiritual Warfare dream—A dream given by God to an individual to highlight demonic strategies and plans for attack upon oneself or another.

Calling dream—A dream given by God to an individual to reveal to them a part of their destiny or calling in life.

Revelatory dream—A dream given by God to an individual that reveals a specific truth He desires for them to respond to in obedience and faith.

Warning dream—A dream given by God to an individual to warn them of a present or future occurrence that will harm them or another physically, emotionally, or spiritually.

Healing dream—A dream given by God to an individual to heal their emotional and spiritual scars related to a difficult time in their life.

Cleansing dream—A dream given by God to an individual to highlight the need for a spiritual cleansing or detoxification that needs to occur in the person's life.

Natural dream—A dream arising out of one's own mind as a normal function of the human brain at rest.

Dark dream—A dream given by demonic forces to an individual for the purposes of deceiving, impeding, or harassing that person.

Uncoded dream—a dream containing no hidden symbols and for which the meaning is immediately clear to the dreamer.

Simple coded dream—a dream containing simple, basic symbols, which upon reflection can be partially decoded by the dreamer.

Complex coded dream—a dream containing deeply cryptic symbols, which upon reflection is difficult for the dreamer to decode.

Gift of Dream Interpretation, the—The unique, God-given ability to decode the symbolism and explain the meaning of dreams and/or visions that others receive from God.

Dream catalog—A compilation of recurring symbols and their meanings, unique to each individual, which is then used to aid that individual in interpreting their dreams.

Dream evangelism—The process of accurately interpreting the dreams of others as a tangible demonstration of God's love, with the end result being an opportunity to share the Gospel of Christ with that person.

Appendix I

A Selection of Biblical Dreams

THE FOLLOWING LIST WILL aid you as you continue your own personal study of dreams and how God used them throughout the Old and New Testaments. Each dream is classified into one of the ten types as discussed in chapter 3.

Reference	Dream	Type
Genesis 15:12–16	Abram foresees Israel's bondage & deliverance	prophetic/ encouragement
Genesis 20:1–7	Abimelech warned not to touch Sarah	warning
Genesis 28:10–16	Jacob sees a stairway to heaven	prophetic/ encouragement
Genesis 31:10–13 (see also Genesis 30:25–43)	Jacob receives insight on how to increase his livestock wealth	revelatory
Genesis 31:22–24	Laban given instructions on how to approach Jacob	revelatory
Genesis 37:5–8	Joseph dreams of sheaves of grain bowing before him	calling/prophetic
Genesis 37:9–11	Joseph dreams the sun, moon, and stars bow before him	calling/prophetic
Genesis 40:1–13	Egyptian cupbearer sees himself serving Pharaoh	prophetic

Genesis 40:16–22	Egyptian baker sees baskets of bread on his head	prophetic
Genesis 41:1–4	Pharaoh dreams of seven sickly cows	prophetic/warning
Genesis 41:5–7	Pharaoh dreams of seven thin heads of grain	prophetic/warning
Judges 7:13–15	A Midianite dreams of a barley loaf	prophetic/spiritual warfare
1 Kings 3:5–15	Solomon is asked a question by God	encouragement/confirmation
Job 4:12–17	Eliphaz receives a message about God's righteousness	revelatory/portrait
Daniel 2:26–47	Nebuchadnezzar dreams of a mighty statue	prophetic
Daniel 4:4–33	Nebuchadnezzar dreams of a massive tree	warning
Daniel 7:1–28	Daniel's vision/dream about four beasts	prophetic
Daniel 8:1–26	Daniel's vision/dream about a ram and a goat	prophetic
Daniel 10:1–21	Daniel's vision/dream about a radiant man in linen	prophetic
Matthew 1:18–24	Joseph is told that Mary is carrying Christ	healing/revelatory
Matthew 2:7–12	The Magi told to not reveal Jesus' whereabouts	warning
Matthew 2:13–15	Joseph told to flee to Egypt with Jesus and Mary	warning
Matthew 2:19–21	Joseph told to return to Israel with Jesus and Mary	revelatory
Matthew 2:22–23	Joseph warned to stay away from Archelaus	warning
Matthew 27:15–19	Pilate's wife dreams of Jesus' innocence	revelatory/confirmation

Appendix II

Questions & Answers

HERE ARE A FEW of the most common questions about dreams. I hope this additional appendix is helpful as you continue your study of spiritual dreams.

I rarely dream, or at least I rarely remember mine. What can I do to start receiving more dreams from God?

God speaks to His children differently. In addition to hearing the Lord from the pages of the Bible, some tend to get inner impressions regularly, others hear Him more clearly from nature or life circumstances, while others often hear the Lord through dreams and visions.

However, I believe the Lord desires to speak to all of His children through dreams from time to time. The best way to see an increase in dreams is to simply ask God for them. If you will obey and respond to the few dreams He does give you, you will see an increase in your level of dreaming.

If you know someone who receives lots of spiritual dreams, then ask them to lay hands on you and pray for more dreams to manifest in your life. I believe strongly in the power of spiritual impartation. The Lord will honor those who hunger to hear Him.

How can I better remember my dreams when I first wake up?

Dreams are written with invisible ink and they fade very quickly upon waking. When you first wake up, meditate on the dream and ask the Lord to help you recall it. Go over what you do remember. Then lay still and quiet, with your eyes closed, and slowly a few more bits and pieces will rise to your consciousness.

Once you have recalled all that you can, replay the entire dream, scene by scene, two or three more times so that it will lodge in your short term memory. Then immediately get out of bed and record it. You'll never remember more of your dream than in those first five minutes after waking. Before you use the bathroom, before you make that first cup of coffee, before you do anything, record the dream. Dream memory is like a muscle. The more you exercise it, the stronger it will become.

I had a dream involving one of the top twenty "common symbols" and the interpretation I felt the Lord gave me didn't match the meaning you gave for that symbol. Is my interpretation wrong?

Absolutely not. Remember, dream symbols are unique to the dreamer. The common symbols I share in the book are accurate about 80 percent of the time but they can certainly mean something different in your dreams. Always go with the confirmation of your own spirit when dealing with dream interpretation. My book, or any other dream interpretation book, is never the final word on a dream symbol's meaning. God reserves the right to make any symbol mean anything He wants in your particular dreams.

I have a recurring dream at least once every few months or every few years. Why do I keep having this same dream over and over?

Recurring dreams take place when there are spiritual, psychological, or emotional scars that have never fully healed. Recurring dreams alert us to areas where closure is needed but has not yet taken place. These dreams will continue to surface until the issue is resolved or you allow God to do spiritual surgery on you and heal the matter once and for all. Sin, abuse, shame, neglect, fear, regret and other negative realities are common causes of recurring dreams.

I've also found it quite common for calling dreams to show up as recurring dreams. The Lord will often give the dreamer the same dream every few years as a reminder that they have not yet embraced a specific aspect of their calling. The Lord also provides recurring portrait dreams to highlight areas of deficiency in our spiritual walk that we need to overcome.

There are times when recurring dreams are positive and the Lord will use the same dream over and over as a way to remind us of some promise He had made to us. More times than not, recurring dreams are negative, not positive, in the dreamer's life. Recurring dreams are usually indicative of an area in our life that needs some work and attention or an issue the Lord has been highlighting to us, but we've not yet fully grasped. Once we have addressed the issue or allowed the Lord to heal that area of our life, then the recurring dream will finally fade away.

When a person I know shows up in my dream, how do I know if the dream is about that person, or if they are just a "type," or if the dream is just highlighting the meaning of their name?

It's not always easy to know. That is why we must depend on the Holy Spirit when it comes to dream interpretation. We simply can't do this mechanically in our own understanding if we want to be truly accurate in our interpretations. The Holy Spirit must reveal to us what the symbols mean and what the person in our dream represents. We can certainly run through which of these three meanings makes the most sense, and sometimes it is obvious, but when it is not immediately apparent we have to ask for divine assistance in the interpretive process.

I sometimes have dreams where a man shows up to help me or guide me but I can never make out his face. It is either blurry, or obscured in some way, or I am positioned in such a way that I can't see his face. Who is this "faceless" man?

This is a common occurrence in spiritual dreams. Very often a faceless man represents the Holy Spirit. The fact that you can't see His face is symbolic of the fact that He has no face, because He is not really a man after all, rather He is the mighty Holy Spirit of God who is sent to guide us, protect us, and lead us into all truth.

If you see a figure who is not faceless, but for some reason you can never quite see his face because it's skewed in some way or at an angle blocking clear recognition, then that is often indicative of an angel.

Sometimes my dreams are not in normal colors but instead are in really dull, muted colors, or in shades of gray. Is there any significance to this?

Oftentimes demonic, dark dreams show up as muted color dreams. Sometimes spiritual dreams will appear this way as well when highlighting issues relating to Satan, his forces, or spiritual warfare issues in general.

Is there any significance to the specific time that one awakens from a spiritual dream?

Most of the time I would say don't concern yourself with the time you wake up from a dream. Concern yourself with the message of the dream. That's what is really important. However, there are times when the Lord will provide you with additional insight based on the specific time He woke you from the dream.

For instance, if you had a dream in which the Lord showed you something great He wanted to do in your life and you are having a hard time believing it could really happen, the dream could be further confirmed due to the fact that you awoke from this encouraging dream at exactly "2:22 am." Why would this be further confirmation? Because "2" is the number of confirmation. The Lord is essentially saying, "I will do this thing in your life. It is confirmed, confirmed, confirmed."

If you were to dream of a co-worker in sin and you awakened with a heavy burden to intercede for this person it would certainly be revealing if you awoke precisely at "3:56 am." Why? Because those numbers could be prophetically stating that, "the Lord will provide grace to overcome this sin." "3" is the number for God. "5" is the number for grace, and "6" is the number for mankind in general, or in this particular dream it would signify its other common meaning of "sin" or "works of the flesh."

Sometimes the Lord will wake you up at a particular time because He wants to highlight a biblical passage that lines up with the exact time He woke you up. For example, one might awaken from a powerful prophetic dream at "5:24 am" and immediately feel led to read the book of I Thessalonians. Opening your Bible to I Thessalonians 5:24, you would find that the verse promises, "The one who calls you is faithful, and he will do it." In this instance the scripture is meant to further reinforce the message of the dream. The Lord is essentially telling you, "What you dreamed about is truly from Me, *and I will do it.*"

So, don't try to force a secondary message into every dream based on what time you woke up. Again, the content of the dream is what is most important. However, be open to the fact that sometimes the exact time you woke up is important. The Lord will let you know when to apply this truth.

Shouldn't we use the Bible as the standard for determining a dream symbol's meaning? If so, why would we ever want to consult a dream dictionary to find a symbol's meaning?

We should absolutely become familiar with the Bible's standard meanings for common symbols, for they will often show up in our dreams. For instance, Jesus Himself is often symbolized by a rock. Water is often symbolic of the Holy Spirit. Knowing these common biblical symbols will be extremely useful when interpreting dreams. The Lord regularly uses these symbols still today.

However, the Lord supplements the symbols in scripture and meets us where we are by speaking to us through symbols that are specific to our particular time and culture. Besides speaking to us through common biblical symbols like rocks, fishing, and farming, He also speaks through modern common objects like cars, airplanes, and skyscrapers.

I believe the Lord has given me the spiritual gift of dream interpretation. Sometimes I get amazing insight into my dreams and the dreams of others, but there are other times when I hear a dream and I struggle to ascertain its meaning. If I have the "gift" of interpreting dreams why can't I interpret every dream brought to me?

It might be helpful to think about the strength of your spiritual gift as operating on a scale of 1 to 10. Just because two people share the same gift does not mean they have the same level of anointing in that gift. The gift of dream interpretation is like any other spiritual gift; there are ranges in skill level. There are those in the body of Christ operating at a level 4, some at level 5 or 6, while others highly developed in their gift may be functioning at a 9 or 10.

The important thing is to exercise your gift faithfully at whatever level you currently operate in. As you are faithful and grow in your relationship with Jesus your gift will strengthen. You may be a 4 today but in the future you may function at a 6 or 7. Remember, God rewards faithfulness and gifts take time to develop.

Appendix III

Reflection Questions for Group Study

Chapter 1: One Dreamer to Another

1. Have you ever had a dream you felt was from God? Did you understand what it meant? Did you act on it? If so, what happened?
2. What has been your attitude toward dreams throughout your life? In a typical week, how often do you dream?
3. What are the benefits of being open to spiritual dreams? What are the consequences of dismissing them?

Chapter 2: A Survey of Dreams Throughout History

4. Why would God give someone a revelation through a dream if there were a chance they would miss its meaning?
5. What kinds of dreams did God give to people in the Old and New Testament? What purposes did they serve?
6. Are dreams and visions supposed to continue throughout the New Testament age until the return of Christ? What passage in the New Testament addresses this?

Chapter 3: What the Bible Teaches about Dreams

7. What are some of the primary ways God speaks to people?

8. What are ten common types of dreams found in scripture? Has God ever given you one of these dreams? If you feel comfortable doing so, share a personal story with the group about your dream, and how God worked in your life through that experience.
9. Does God only speak to Christians in spiritual dreams?
10. Do all Christians receive spiritual dreams? Is there a correlation between your walk with God and the frequency of your dreams?

Chapter 4: Why God Speaks in Mysteries and Symbols

11. Describe the differences between an uncoded, simple coded, and complex coded dream.
12. Why is revelation from God not always clear and obvious? What might be the reason behind God's use of symbols, parables, and riddles?
13. Read Numbers 12:6–8 and Matthew 13:10–17. Discuss the concept of progressive revelation. Why does God veil revelation? Is there a correlation between our walk with the Lord and our ability to hear Him and receive revelatory insight from heaven?

Chapter 5: Natural Dreams, Spiritual Dreams, Dark Dreams

14. What's the difference between a natural dream and a spiritual dream?
15. How can we be sure a spiritual dream is really from God? How can such a dream be tested?
16. Can a Christian receive a dark dream? Why or why not?

Chapter 6: Principles for Successful Dream Interpretation

17. What are some common word devices and coded language phenomena that appear regularly in dreams?
18. This book cautions us about putting too much faith into standard dream dictionaries to arrive at the meaning of our

Reflection Questions For Group Study

dream symbols. What is the reason for this conclusion? Do you agree or disagree?
19. What is a dream catalog? If you can, share with the group some symbols from your personal dream catalog and what they mean to you.

Chapter 7: Common Symbols in Spiritual Dreams

20. What are some common dream symbols for God, heaven, or holiness?
21. What are some common dream symbols for evil, sin, or demonic forces?
22. What do houses often symbolize in dreams? Share what the following rooms of a house might symbolize in dream form: living room, kitchen, roof, attic, basement, closet, bedroom, and bathroom.
23. Can colors and numbers have spiritual significance? If so, list three numbers and three colors that often appear in dreams and discuss their possible spiritual associations.

Chapter 8: Inviting God into the World of Your Dreams

24. Can we ask God to give us spiritual dreams? Why or why not?
25. Why is it important to journal and to keep a log of our spiritual dreams?

Chapter 9: Protocol for Dream Interpreters

26. Why is it important for some dream interpretations to be recorded?
27. Would it ever be proper for an interpreter to withhold some part of the dream's interpretation from the dreamer? Why or why not?
28. How important is it for the dream interpreter to be submitted to spiritual authority in their own life? What ministry

temptations are common in those with the gift of dream interpretation?

Chapter 10: Case Studies: 7 Dreams Decoded

29. Which of these dreams was the easiest for you to decode? Which one was the most difficult?
30. When reading over the seven dreams, did God give you any additional insights on the meaning of these dreams or for particular parts of any dream?

Notes

Chapter 2: Dreams Throughout History

1. Ward Hill Lamon, *Recollections of Abraham Lincoln 1847–1865* (Lincoln: University of Nebraska Press, 1994), 116–117.
2. Raphael, *The Royal Book of Dreams From an Ancient and Curious Manuscript* (London: E. Wilson, 1830); www.chestofbooks.com/new-age/dreams/Royal-Dream-Book/index.html, accessed June 14, 2010.
3. Caroline Finkel, *Osman's Dream* (New York: Basic Books, 2005), xiii; Edward Shepherd Creasy, *Turkey: The History of Nations* (Nabu Press, 2010), 15; Mehmet Fuad Koprulu, *The Origins of the Ottoman Empire* (New York: State University of New York Press, 1992).
4. Otto Loewi, "Uber humorale Ubertragbarkeit der Herznervenwirkung" *Pflugers Archives,* 189, pp. 239–242; T.N. Raju, "The Nobel Chronicles. 1936: Henry Hallett Dale (1875–1968) and Otto Loewi (1873–1961)" *Lancet 353* (9150); 416, January 30, 1999; Otto Loewi, "An Autobiographical Sketch," *Perspectives in Biology and Medicine,* Autumn, 1960.
5. "Frederick Grant Banting (1891–1941), Co-discoverer of Insulin," *Journal of the American Medical Association* (November 1966), 198 (6): 660–1; www.kosmix.com/topic/frederick_banting, accessed July 7, 2010.
6. Richard Rhodes, *The Making of the Atomic Bomb* (New York: Simon and Schuster, 1986), 62–63; www.luciddreamlessons.

com/2009/03/04/incredible-famous-dreams, accessed July 3, 2010; David Favrholdt, *Niels Bohr's Philosophical Background* (Copenhagen: Munksgaard, 1992), 42–63.
7. Jeremy Taylore, *Dream Work* (Mahway, NJ: Paulist Press, 1983).
8. Roger G. Swearingen, *The Prose Writings of Robert Louis Stevenson* (London: Macmillan, 1980), 37; William Gray, *Robert Louis Stevenson: A Literary Life* (New York: Palgrave Macmillan, 2004); *Nightmare: Birth of Victorian Horror* (1966 British Broadcasting Corporation television series).
9. A'Lelia P. Bundles, *On Her Own Ground: The Life and Times of Madam C.J. Walker* (New York: Lisa Drew Books/Scribner, 2001); www.MadamecjWalker.com, accessed June 25, 2010; Kathy Reiss, *Hope in a Jar: The Making of America's Beauty Culture* (New York: Owl Books/Henry Holt & Company, 1999).
10. Waldemar, Kaempffert, ed., *A Popular History of American Invention,* Vol. II (New York: Scribner's Sons, 1924); "A Brief History of the Sewing Machine," ISMACS International, accessed June 17, 2010; "Sewing Machine History," Machine- History.com, accessed June 18, 2010; George Iles, *Leading American Inventors* (New York: Henry Holt Company, 1910), 338–369.
11. Morton Kelsey, *God, Dreams, and Revelation* (Minneapolis: Augsburg Fortress, 1991), 106.
12. Thomas O'Loughlin, *Discovering Saint Patrick* (New York: Paulist Press, 2005), 149- 150.
13. Liam De Paor, *Saint Patrick's World: The Christian Culture of Ireland's Apostolic Age* (Dublin: Four Courts Press, 1993), 100.
14. Catherine Swift, *John Newton* (Minneapolis: Bethany House Publishers, 1991), 38–39.
15. John Dunn, *A Biography of John Newton* (Adelaide and Sydney, Australia: New Creation Teaching Ministry, 1994), 5; John Newton, *The Works of John Newton,* Vol. 1 (Edinburgh, Scotland: Banner of Truth Trust, 1985), 8.

Chapter 5: Natural Dreams, Spiritual Dreams, Dark Dreams

16. Kelly Bulkeley, *An Introduction to the Psychology of Dreaming* (Westport, Connecticut: Praeger Publishers, 1997), 53–54.

Milton Keynes UK
Ingram Content Group UK Ltd.
UKHW021316301024
2472UKWH00058B/789